The COMPLETE BOOK *of* MOUNTAIN BIKING

The COMPLETE BOOK of MOUNTAIN BIKING

BRANT RICHARDS
& STEVE WORLAND

Introduction by
GARY FISHER

HarperCollins*Publishers*

For information, address
HarperCollins Publishers, Inc.,
10 East 53rd Sreet, New York, NY 10022

HarperCollins books may be purchased for educational,
business, or sales promotional use. For information,
please write: Special Markets Department,
HarperCollins Publishers, Inc.,
10 East 53rd Sreet, New York, NY 10022

Library of Congress Cataloging-in-Publication Data
Richards, Brant.
The Complete Book of Mountain Biking/Brant Richards
& Steve Worland
       p.   cm.
ISBN 0–06–273027–4
1. All terain cycling.   I. Worland, Steve. II Title.
GV1056.R53   1997   97-7400
796.6'3– –dc21   CIP

The Authors assert the moral right to be
identified as the authors of this work.

Designed and produced by **Cooling Brown**
Hampton, Middlesex, England

Art Direction: *Arthur Brown*
Senior Editor: *Ann Kay*
Consultant Editor: *Dan Hope*
Design: *Tish Mills, Alistair Plumb*
Technical Assistant: *William Burdis*

Colour reproduction by
Saxon Photolitho, Norwich, England

CONTENTS

I think it was H.G. Wells who once said "When I see an adult on a bicycle I have hope for the human race." It kinda sums up the ground rules of my own driving force. I've been into bikes since I was a small kid. I'm a big kid now and nothing's really changed in the wide scheme of things.

INTRODUCTION

by GARY FISHER

The bicycle, until this last decade or so, has just been undercover. It's been hiding out, camouflaging its true colors, disguising its role. I would like to propose that a bicycle (and especially a mountain bike) is one of the best-conceived but most disgracefully underrated gifts to human society in the twentieth century. In a world where so many of our consumer products are simply ill-conceived exercises in hi-jinks marketing prowess, the mountain bike is a breath of fresh mountain air. It's a truly remarkable invention, because it's brought the bicycle out of the closet. Mr. Wells hit the nail on the head, but I'd prefer to be more specific. When I see a man, a woman or a child on a mountain bike, I too have hope for the human race.

So when did it all start? Well it all depends on whether you're talking about off-roading or mountain biking. People have been riding bikes off-road since... well, since before roads were built. When the single-speed beach cruisers took off way back in the forties, I'm sure no one would have guessed where we'd end up half a century later. I really loved all those early balloon-tired monsters. We called them ballooners, then later klunkers — I guess because of the noise those fenders made as soon as you rode over anything vaguely bumpy. They were the very antithesis of cycling as a sport. The racers rode skinnies. For everyone else it was the fatter the better. Fat tires meant more comfort. Less speed on black-top with all that drag and excessive weight, but more comfort. Luxus!

The sixties and seventies changed things round a bit, first for me then slowly but surely for the rest of the world of bicycling. I'd always been big into the speed thing on bikes. I was racing bikes as early as '62, doing road, track and cyclo-cross. In '64 I got second in the Intermediate Northern California Road Championships. Then the sixties kinda got in the way and I was growing my hair and doing light shows for bands. It was a great time. I got to do some cool innovation with the light show stuff. It

taught me things about lateral thinking. Later, when I got back into bikes, those sideways thought processes started to take me places. Places in races, places in time and places in method. I guess the whole mountain bike thing might not have happened the way it did if it wasn't for all those great learning years at the end of the sixties.

Anyhow, I got back into biking again, racing on the road, doing 200 to 500 miles a week and winning stuff at weekends. I strung together a few part-time jobs. I helped out with the wrenching in local bike stores and with more than enough time to sleep, play, eat, work and ride, I just went from strength to strength. Life was sweet.

THIS COULD BE THE START OF SOMETHING BIG

A bunch of friends used to go out and ride their klunkers down the local hills. Did I say ride? Okay, they hammered. They flew. They crashed. And they freewheeled most of the time because the trails they chose only went down. They usually went down with a vengeance. They had to push those heavy machines to the top or, if someone happened by in a pickup, they hitched a ride. The bikes often got trashed on the way down. They were heavily built monsters but everything has its limits.

I joined them for a few rides. I loved those bikes. We'd trash them, then we'd pick up another one for five dollars in a junk store. Whenever we went out, half of us would have to walk home carrying the remains of the latest casualty. There were a few human casualties too. A flesh wound or two was just a part of the game. Slowly the bikes started to get better. I started shopping for motorcycle parts, strengthening stuff. The thing that always bugged me was that we couldn't ride back uphill.

I got to thinking. All I needed to do was to build a bike that wouldn't fall apart on the downs and that could be pedalled back to the top. I was fit enough. I just needed a good ride position and some decent gears. It didn't take long to put something together. I modified my old classic, a '38 Schwinn Excelsior X clunker. I put a triple crankset on the front and five cogs on the back. I used long cranks instead of the shorties the other guys were using. It weighed 41lb but I was strong enough to get it up almost anything, and it seemed like this was the first klunker that didn't fall apart. I took it out to Colorado and rode a 13,000-foot pass. Up and down! At the time I didn't realize that this was to become the turning point. The start of something big? Hell, I had no idea; just lots of ideas.

THE SPIRIT OF THE BIKE

We've come a long way since those early days. The 'mountain bike' tag is something of a misnomer for many of today's riders, but it's a tag that stuck for obvious reasons. It has a ring to it, an air of adventure, daring and achievement. Everyone's looking for stuff like that these days.

We live in a high-pressure world. Everyone feels that, from kids to high-power business types. The mountain bike can go a heap further than simply suggesting release from the pressures. It will actually take you out there, on a whim, a wing and a prayer. It will get your body working. It will challenge your initiative. It will teach you that real mechanical excellence can be easy to comprehend if you just give it a chance. Stuff like that can revitalize the human spirit in a way that very few other inanimate objects can achieve. I have to keep reminding myself that the mountain bike is an inanimate object, because when I ride it feels like anything but. My relationship with my bike is a lot like a love affair. I treat it well, I miss it when I'm away, I respect its limitations and it's usually real good to me in return.

THE CHILD IN US ALL

Kids love bikes too. In fact, kids love bikes for the same reasons as the rest of us. Think about all those reasons and suddenly we're all kids on bikes again. Bikes are great fun, and many other things besides. They're status objects. They're utilitarian work tools. Perhaps above all they're vehicles that greatly enhance the feeling of physical independence and emotional release from the rigors of organized life. And the mountain bike is the best bike of all. It truly frees the human spirit.

Until we can return to the days of safe roads, the kids, and other bike novices, have to learn their bike skills on the trail. The mountain bike has made that task much easier than it was in pre-mountain bike days. It's made biking much easier for everyone. Now a whole generation of non-cyclists have an opportunity to get into bikes without the grind and hassle of traffic. One of the main reasons for the massive growth in the popularity of mountain bikes is the fact that they're far easier, far safer and therefore far more fun to ride than other bikes.

We all like coming together with like-minded groups and achieving something. Groups of kids on bikes can achieve to

their hearts' content. They create challenges, they learn body coordination skills, they solve technical problems and they construct all sorts of games. The distance they can travel relates to all the other skills that continue to develop as the bike becomes more and more an enhancement of physical being. Think about this. It's basic stuff, and it applies to all of us. What are we if not grown-up kids?

Road traffic has become the single most disabling factor to the logical development of getting about by bike, but the advent of the mountain bike has meant that we can realize all our basic needs away from the traffic-afflicted hassles of modern living. We can discover the joys of cycling that existed before roads became battlegrounds. We can find out about the bits of the planet that really matter. Sure, we all have a modern life to deal with too, but it's good to know that we can escape for a while without always waiting for the vacation.

I guess all this stuff is why it still gives me a boost whenever I see someone on a bike. The novelty, the expectation and the hope of an inspiring future of bike-influenced society will never wear thin. Hey, it is still getting me smiling after all these years.

ROSY FUTURE

People keep asking me what I think about bikes for the future. The 'tech head' in me sees all sorts of interesting stuff happening to bike design. The spiritual head is more concerned with how bikes need to be sucked into town planning. The tech head sees beauty in the technical fix. The spiritual head looks for social and political change. The big picture is that bikes will continue to evolve in both technical and social terms. I guess that has to be good for riders and for our society as a whole. The real interesting stuff is trying to work out all that fine detail of how the evolution will actually happen.

The mountain bike has been the biggest thing to happen to bikes since way back when someone added pedals to the hobby horse. Mountain bikes were not just evolution. They were a revolution, and one that I am proud to have played an active part in. Even in a time before the salad days of the infernal combustion engine, bike sales could only ever grow gently. For most folks, getting a bike, in disposable income terms, used to be like getting a car is to most folks these days. The bike thing grew but then the car thing grew more and bikes dwindled again as a result.

These days, bikes are growing faster

than cars. Cars have closed in on their saturation point in some places. Cars in their present form are a threat to the human scale of modern societies, and that's too high a price to pay. The growing congestion and the pollution problems mean that cars have passed their peak in terms of use value. Now you're far more likely to overhear conversations about which mountain bike to buy than which car. Even in many 'first world' countries, sales of bikes are outnumbering sales of cars — and most of those sales are mountain bikes.

So how's it going to go in the future then? Man, I'm no prophet. I really don't know, but I do have a few thoughts on the subject. I guess the whole sport angle on the mountain bike thing is a reflection of the extremes. Downhill racing and cross-country racing have moved further and further apart. Cross-country bikes stress light weight, immediate handling responses and speed related to rider pedal-power. Downhill bikes stress damage limitation through big shock absorption, skills-related speed and, it can't be denied, a degree of attitude that emerges from a willingness to take calculated risks for the sake of thrills.

Somewhere in between those two bike types lies the most likely future of the average Joe's mountain bike. Take a few aspects of the lightweight approach, a few aspects of the damage limitation approach, concentrate on comfort and ride posture for ease of skills building and you'll end up with somewhere near the perfect utilitarian fun bike. It won't be the lightest bike out there, and it won't guarantee to shrug off high-speed incidents with large boulders, but it will allow a rider, any rider, to progress quickly in everything that a bike should represent: transport, fun, skills development, intuition, sociability, thrills and, last but not least, that all-important feel good factor.

GETTING SORTED

You don't need to own a top of the line machine to score that feel good thing, or for any of the other good stuff that comes from biking. All you need is a bike that fits. Mountain bikes, and other bikes, are becoming increasingly categorized by rider type and preferred terrain type. That's not necessarily a good thing. Sure, local terrain will vary, but mountain bikes should be capable of tackling pretty much anything you point them at, within the bounds of reason and rider ability.

In theory, it's easy to decide what sort of rider you are and what sort of riding you expect to do. Then you can decide what

kind of bike you need. In practice, many mountain bikers will find themselves being increasingly drawn to much more challenging terrain, the type that an absolute beginner bike might struggle to conquer. Even when you think you'll be riding mainly hardpack trails and black-top, a compromise road / off-road bike or a bike that's simply too damn cheap could hinder your ambitions. So get a 'real' mountain bike. Hey, you can always fit those skinny treads if you end up riding road all the time. And you can always upgrade to a bouncy fork if a rigid one limits your aims.

For me, a 'real' mountain bike can be anything from an entry-level chromoly steel-framed rigid mount to a dual-suspension aluminum job with bells and whistles componentry. Essentially, the two bikes do the same job. You'll learn to appreciate the expensive super-scoot more if you learn all the groundwork on the cheap one. I guess we all know that our purchase choices are driven by more than just pure practicality and common sense. Do you really need those flashy Nike Airs for walking to the stores? It's the same with bikes. The bike you choose to buy should suit your ego and your ambition as well as your wallet.

This book is about all the things you'll need to know in order to get fully involved

GARY FISHER

in mountain biking, from getting started to advanced trail techniques, holidays with altitude, racing, looking after your bike and getting the best out of your rides. Where I've come from, bike riders become mountain bikers because they develop an attitude. That attitude encompasses the bike, the rides, the ground we ride on, the language we speak to one another and the air we breathe. Riding a mountain bike is an inspiring preoccupation. I hope that what we're saying in these pages will inspire those who are still sending out exploratory tentacles into our world. Come on in. You're very welcome.

CHAPTER ONE

Mountain bike anatomy

Mountain biking has become a hot-bed of cycling design. The enthusiasm with which mountain bikers have accepted the sport means that far more development has gone into mountain bikes in the last twenty years than in the last hundred years of road bikes. Many of the developments — suspension systems, advanced wheel and rim designs, alternative braking systems and use of new materials — are appearing on road bikes, and there's now quite a lot to learn...

The mountain bike

A mountain bike might look like any other sort of bike (two wheels, handlebars, pedals, brakes) but each of its components are far, far stronger — to cope with the bumps and impacts that are a regular part of off-road riding. Its frame is stronger, its brakes more powerful, its gears offer a wider range. Read on to find out more.

A mountain bike is basically a frame, which comes in different materials and shapes, with other components attached to it. That frame may incorporate a rear-suspension system and it may have certain components fitted to suit the bike's specific use. Downhillers will need long-travel suspension forks, big tires and disc brakes, while a cross-country racer wants a light bike, with fast, hard tires, a short-travel suspension fork and a riding position more like that of a road bike.

The combinations of components, and the resulting combinations of bikes that can be built, are almost limitless. However, we'll now attempt to guide you through the basic types of frame and component.

THE FRAME

Though some material (notably carbon fiber) can be built into frames without the use of actual tubes, most mountain bikes are built from tubes. These are then welded or bonded together to form a frame. The different options follow below.

THE MODERN MOUNTAIN BIKE
Typical of its kind, this is a traditional double-triangle frame, with conventionally spoked wheels. It's a fairly straightforward design, as you'll soon see...

seat post

front derailleur

frame size

820

cogs

chainrings

rear derailleur

STEEL FRAME

Steel is a truly wonderful material. In this time of high-tech aerospace materials, which aren't improving noticeably in price or performance, steel continues improving quietly in the corner, by itself. The reason for this is that steel is tough and really easy to work with, and there are so many people around who are very, very good at working with it. You don't need plasma welders, ultra-clean environments or funny glues to stick together a steel bike.

High-strength steel tubing comes from extremely specialized factories, where the end product is carefully monitored for the highest quality and to ensure it's strong enough to use in high-stress applications such as bicycles.

Steel tubing doesn't have to be a straight bit of round tube. It is usually 'butted' – made so that the walls are thinner in the center than at the ends. The ends are the most stressed parts of the tube. They're also the place where the tube is welded or 'brazed' to other frame tubes, and the heat required for this may weaken them even further (welding is melting two materials; brazing is melting a filler material between two other materials).

Tubes may also be flared, oval, bulging or flattened, to make them the best shape for the situation they'll be used in.

Tube manufacturers can also thicken parts of the walls to maximize strength in specific areas.

The down side of steel is that, when you're trying to make a very light tube for a super-light frame, the tube's walls may be so thin that they're susceptible to denting or crumpling. Very light frames can be built using steel, but there are other materials more suited to weight-critical applications.

ALUMINUM FRAME

Aluminum was the first frame material to appear in mountain biking as an alternative to steel. Riders who were used to the looks of skinny-framed steel bikes thought that the aluminum frames were fat and ugly, but just one ride proved their worth. Stiff

stem

headset

rim

front forks

spoke

drop-out

standover height

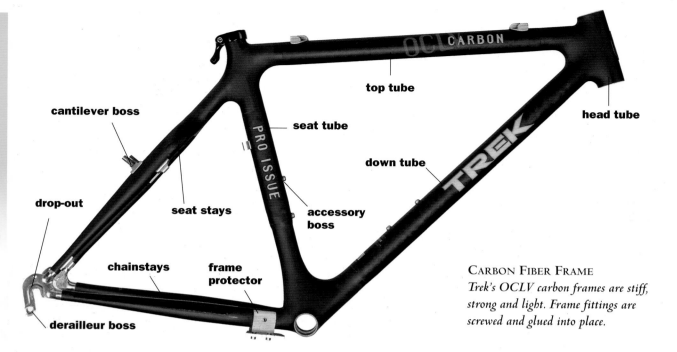

cantilever boss

top tube

seat tube

head tube

down tube

drop-out

seat stays

accessory boss

chainstays

frame protector

derailleur boss

CARBON FIBER FRAME
Trek's OCLV carbon frames are stiff, strong and light. Frame fittings are screwed and glued into place.

on the climbs, comfy on the wash board, and lighter than anyone could believe.

Technology has moved on since those early frames. 6061-T6 was the only tubing available to builders then, in specific sizes and configurations. A giant leap forward for mass production came a couple of years ago, when Easton started producing actual tube sets for aluminum frames, rather than just cutting up lengths of aircraft tube. The difference was the same as that between a straight-gauge steel bike and a double-butted frame. Lighter, stronger (due to correct metal placement) and far comfier to ride.

Aluminum frames are so light because the material is one-third the density of steel. But it's also only one-third the rigidity and one-third the strength, so aluminum tubes for bike frames are made with much larger diameters than steel ones. With aluminum, main triangle tubing

diameters are usually up to 1½in (4cm) and over – a good ¼in (0.5cm) larger than steel tubes.

Aluminum is now the material of choice for full-suspension bikes, where its ease of construction and easy-machining properties have proved invaluable. It builds into a very rigid frame that works well with suspension, but even for rigid-framed bikes, it's still an excellent material to consider; a little more expensive than steel, but lighter and building into a stiffer, more efficient frame set.

TITANIUM FRAME

Titanium frames have actually been around for a long time, but their

incredible cost has kept them out of most riders' reach. Used in most weight-critical, cost-no-object structures – such as light spacecraft and airplanes – titanium has one of the highest strength-to-weight ratios of any material.

The big problem with titanium is that it reacts violently to oxygen when it is welded. It's this difficulty, plus the cost of extracting the raw materials, that make the price so high.

The up side is weight. Even the heaviest titanium frame weighs perhaps ½lb (0.25kg) less than the lightest steel frame, and offers much greater strength. As with aluminum, the lightness of

SINGLE TUBE CONSTRUCTION

The company GT have brought Single Tube Construction to the bicycle market with their STS frames. The bikes are made from thermoplastic rope, heated in a mould to 500°F and blown out to shape with an inflated bladder. It is then cooled and made into a frame. This is a material-specific technique that can only be used on thermoplastic – so there's little point in looking out for a Single-tube blow-moulded steel frame.

titanium frames has its limits, governed by the thinness of the tubing. The tubes must be a certain diameter to be strong enough, and thinning the walls (just like steel) means that they are more susceptible to crumpling.

COMPOSITE FRAME

Using knitted carbon fibers, nylons, glass fibers and other materials, very lightweight frames can be constructed by a variety of means. Typically, carbon fiber frames were built using a technique similar to that of glass-fiber construction – a mat of the material is first soaked in resin to shape it and then cured in an oven. This process is used either for the whole frame or for individual tubes. It's still a mainstream construction technique, but the newest process in composite construction is that of thermoplastics. Here, carbon fibers are combined with a mouldable nylon to form a high-strength 'knitted' material that is used with CNC-machined lugs to form a frame. Thermoplastics are molded when they're heated, while the more traditional type of carbon fiber is a thermoset, which sets to a rigid form when the resin is cured from the fibers. Thermoplastic frames are made by heating a composite sock (a tube made of a carbon fiber and nylon mix) and then applying pressure from a silicone bladder (like a balloon) to press the material into a mold, forming the frame's shape. This type of composite construction has a higher degree of impact resistance than thermoset (regular) carbon fiber construction, though frames built from it aren't as light.

JOINING TUBES

Of course, it's no use having a set of tubes on their own – they need to be joined together to form a frame. And all the right parts need to be welded on to allow you to attach brakes, pedals and gears.

TIG WELDING

Nowadays, TIG welding is the most common way to join metal tubes together. Tungsten Inert Gas Welding is its proper name, and it signifies that the welding torch uses a tungsten tip to apply a super-high electric current to the weld site. This melts the two tubes, while the inert gas (usually argon) is sprayed at the joint, to avoid any oxidization. Steel, aluminum and titanium tubes are joined in this way. The benefits are the speed of the operation, the fact that the weld can be done several times over, and the lack of cleaning up that's necessary afterwards.

However, there are problems. Welding necessitates a high temperature. These high temperatures affect the structure of the metal, making the mechanical properties change. TIG welding can cause stress to become concentrated around the joint edge, in the area

TIG-welded joint

already weakened by applying heat. Smart builders use gussets to distribute the stress evenly around the surface of the tube, stopping all of it from migrating to one point and causing the frame to fail.

Aluminum tubing doesn't just get its strength from the alloys and elements in the metal. Frames are heat- or age-treated after welding to allow the metal to increase in strength. This must be done after welding, to allow the material to recoup its strength, or the frames would quickly fail at the joints.

Titanium frames are the trickiest of all to weld. If molten titanium is exposed to oxygen, it will oxidize, contaminating the whole joint and ruining the frame. This means that titanium frames must be welded in extremely clean conditions, with the tubes filled with inert argon gas and the whole joint very carefully prepared. During the welding process, the whole weld-area must be flooded with more argon. This is expensive and the metal itself is also very difficult to weld, so there is a high labor cost for these frames. Also, if a joint is ruined, the frame has to be scrapped.

BONDING

Several manufacturers bond their frames, and other components. Used notably in carbon fiber construction, bonding is simply a bike-business word for glueing. Extremely high-tech glue is used, then the parts are cured at a high temperature. The great advantage of glueing is that it allows dissimilar materials to be joined. It's impossible, for example, to weld an aluminum drop-out into a carbon fiber frame-tube, but with the right adhesive and joint construction, the bonded joint can be as strong as a weld could ever be.

Braking systems

Mountain bikes were made to go fast. But it's also important to have brakes to stop the things too! Early on in their development, the cantilever brake was established as a standard for mountain bikes and, although it has gone through much development, is still around today. As the bike has developed other, more powerful brakes have appeared, such as hydraulic units and disc brakes.

brake lever

barrel adjuster

brake cable

straddle cable

cantilever brake

brake pads

Most mountain bike brakes are of the cantilever design. They operate by a lever at the handlebar pulling a cable through stiff outer cable to the brake. The two brake arms are connected by a straddle cable, and by pulling on the center of this, both brakes hit the rim and the bike slows down.

It's a simple system, and one that works well, although, with the braking surface being so close to the ground (as it rotates), the brake's performance decreases noticeably in the wet, and the pads can get clogged by mud. Manufacturers have spent a lot of time refining brake pad materials and improving the leverage available, but the big leap forward came in 1996, when Shimano introduced their V brake.

Borrowing a design first seen on hand-made US brakes, they did away with a straddle cable and simply fed the brake cable through one extended cantilever arm to the other. This increased power, provided a more linear brake pull,

BRAKE ASSEMBLY
Most mountain bikes use simple, cable-activated brakes to achieve their superb stopping power.

and got us all stopping faster. Indeed, the design is so simple, and works so well, it seems unlikely that short-arm cantilevers with straddle cables will be around at all in the future. Very few manufacturers are specifying anything other than V-style brakes on their mid- and top of the line bikes.

Other manufacturers have launched their own designs, and it seems that the new standard is the direct-pull V brake style cantilever.

Best of all is the fact that the V brake is much easier to fit to suspension forks and rear-suspension bikes, as its guide tube does away with the need for a cable stop on the frame.

HYDRAULIC BRAKES

Replacing the pulling of cable with the pushing of incompressible fluid, hydraulic brakes have a sealed system, which means less maintenance time. One of the nicest features of the system is the way in which the pads can be popped into the brake unit quickly, and popped out again when they're worn – or if you want to change them to suit a specific trail condition.

The German company Magura™ are at the forefront of hydraulic brake design with their Hydro-stop system, which has been around for many years now. One of the reasons why riders find hydraulic brakes so attractive is that the unit requires no servicing, and that, once again, cable routing is hassle-free. The power available at the rim is slightly less than the modern variety of super-powerful cantilevers, but the clean lines of the cable routing, and the reliability of the sealed system, mean that these brakes are still remarkably popular.

DISC BRAKES

The disc brake consists of a disc, mounted onto a specially made hub, and a brake caliper that is fixed to the frame or fork. The

DISC BRAKE
Hydraulically or cable-operated, these offer the ultimate in braking power.

system used to push the pads onto the disc is usually hydraulic, although cable-operated versions are available. Using much harder pads, running much closer to the disc, the braking power is superb, and barely affected by water or mud. The braking force that can be applied is so powerful that the bike can be slowed down with just one finger. Over the last couple of years, disc brakes have become standard issue for world-class downhill racing, though some of the thunder has been stolen from them because of Shimano™'s V brake.

HYDRAULIC BRAKE
Instead of using wire cables, these brakes are activated hydraulically. They are very powerful and require little maintenance.

Drive-train and wheels

The forward motion of a bike depends on the drive efficiency of the cranks, the cogs, the chainrings and the chain. Collectively, these components are known as the drive-train.

CRANKS

These fit to the bottom bracket axle on a four-faced taper, a peculiar system of linking components that isn't seen in any other mechanical device. It doesn't even work especially well. The four-faced taper is cheap to make, and reasonably simple. Shimano have introduced a new splined bottom bracket axle at the very top end of their product line, and that is expected to gain currency over the next few years. (A splined axle

is one with lots of teeth, as opposed to the four sides of a four-sided axle. One part of the splined axle is toothed and a second part fits over these teeth.)

Cranks are usually made from cold-forged aluminum, but other designs, such as machined aluminum or even welded tubular steel, are now becoming more

common. The chainrings fit to the crank by means of a 'spider,' a four- or five-armed plate that holds all the chainrings.

CHAIN

A mountain bike chain is only slightly different from the chain used on any other bike. Because of the high torque loadings passing

OVERVIEW

The drive-train of the modern mountain bike. Three chainrings at the front, with up to eight cogs at the rear, give twenty four available gears.

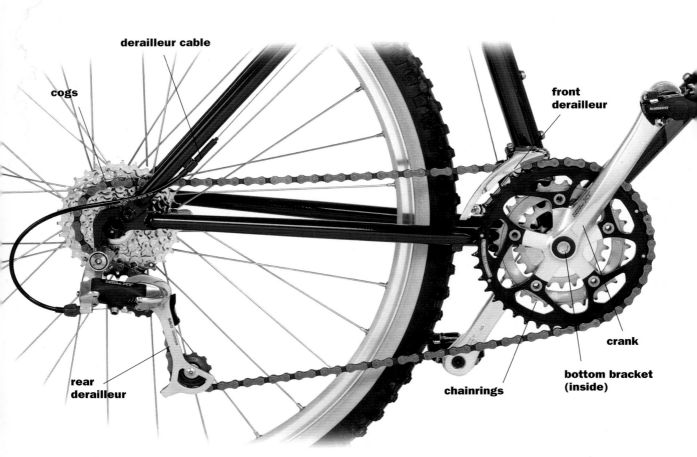

derailleur cable

cogs

front
derailleur

rear
derailleur

chainrings

bottom bracket
(inside)

crank

through a mountain bike drive-train, the chain typically has rivetted joining pins, which ensure that it doesn't split apart under heavy use. Regrettably, this makes removing the chain for cleaning something of a difficult task, involving special re-installation pins and a dose of attention to detail. The pitch and size of the chain is the same as that on any other geared bicycle, except for the very newest 9-speed models.

BOTTOM BRACKET

This bearing unit consists of the bottom bracket axle, with tapered ends that fit snugly into the mating tapers on the cranks, and bearing units that sit inside the bottom bracket cups, which in turn are screwed into the frame. Nowadays, most bottom brackets use free-floating cartridge bearings, and aren't user-serviceable. Fit them, forget them, then throw them away when they're broken.

GEARS

The gear system of a mountain bike is a complex, yet archaic, system of levers, cable and pivoting linkages. Pushing or twisting the shifter at the handlebar pulls a pre-set length of cable through the outer cables on the frame, causing the gear mechanism (derailleur) to move. This pushes on the chain, which then moves from one cog to another. At the front of the bike you've got a triple crank set, and at the back a cluster of five, six, seven or eight cogs. This gives a total of fifteen, eighteen, twenty one or twenty four possible gear ratios.

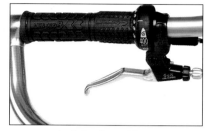

twist-grip shifter

SHIFTERS

There are three types of shifter available at present. The simplest is the thumb shifter, a lever that has an indented stop for each gear (typically seven or eight on the rear derailleur, and three on the front derailleur). Pushing the lever pulls the cable through and makes the derailleur select the right gear. Pulling the lever releases the cable and lets the derailleur drop back to smaller cogs. Then there are the trigger-systems, of which the most popular is Shimano's Rapid Fire system. These operate like the trigger on a gun. Pushing the shift levers pulls or releases the derailleur cable, but the shift levers return to the same position after every

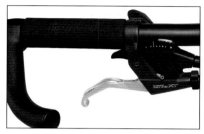

trigger shift

change. The other type available is the twist-grip shifter, where the cable is pulled round the barrel of the shifter, like the throttle on a motorbike.

Each system has its own proponents. Twist-grip shifters are the lightest and the simplest to use, but trigger-shifters work the fastest and are better for experienced riders. Thumb shifters are now in decline, due to the newer systems.

DERAILLEURS

The units that actually do the changing of the gears are pretty standard, right across all cycling. They are called 'derailleurs,' a use of the French word, because they 'de-rail' the chain so that it shifts from cog to cog. Compared to road bikes, the derailleurs used on mountain bikes are typically a little stronger, sealed more effectively against the elements and also larger — to allow

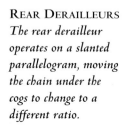

REAR DERAILLEURS
The rear derailleur operates on a slanted parallelogram, moving the chain under the cogs to change to a different ratio.

PEDALS

The earliest mountain bikes simply used the biggest, gnarliest pedals going. Nowadays, many mountain bikers use clipless pedals, which consist of a metal plate bolted to the sole of a cycling shoe, and a catch mechanism built into the pedal. Some downhill riders use flat pedals with vicious spikes to grip onto their shoes.

CLIPLESS PEDALS
These first appeared on road bikes, designed by a company called Look, who developed the click-in pedals from ski boot bindings. Until the click-in (or clipless) pedal arrived, riders who wanted their feet to stay in the pedals had to use toe straps, clips and metal cleats that locked them firmly into the pedal. Clipless pedals allowed solid pedaling efficiency, but with the option of releasing easily, simply by twisting your heels outward.

Shimano brought the clipless pedal to mountain biking with their SPD system. Instead of the large plastic cleat as used on the Look system, SPD shoes had a small steel cleat bolted to them. The pedals, though complicated, were tough enough to stand up to being smashed on rocks and stomped through the mud. Clipless pedals made riding off-road easier. Crashes are fewer and the bike can be maneuvered more easily.

FLAT PEDALS
When you're really riding hard in extreme terrain, it makes a lot of sense not to be secured to your pedals at all. If you need to get a foot down, riding with big, flat pedals means that nothing gets in your way when you need to make a corrective dab. However, even in extreme downhill competition, these pedals are being replaced by pedals that offer a clipless center, but have a heavily spiked cage to rest on when you're not clipped in.

CLIPS AND STRAPS
Many bikes are sold with clips and straps, and they do a good, budget-priced job of keeping your feet on the pedals. Toe clips also allow you to get out of the pedals easily, a skill that's learned quickly with clipless pedals, but one that people aren't always happy with.

them to cope with the greater extremes of gears that mountain bikes have.

Derailleurs are 'cages' mounted on parallelogram-shaped linkages that allow them to track closely to the chainrings or cogs. Changing gear is simply a matter of pushing the chain from one cog to the next – crude, but efficient. Manufacturers have designed cogs and chainrings with pick-up and release teeth to ease the progress of the chain, but it's still a pretty crude system.

The neatest systems around are those that use internally geared hubs to offer six or seven speeds without the need for a rear cassette. Unfortunately, these are also extremely heavy.

WHEELS
Road bike wheels are delicate. The thin rubber tires and skinny rims look as if they'll barely stand up to any impact at all. Mountain bike wheels are actually only slightly heavier than road bike wheels – the spoked wheel itself is an immensely strong structure, and the fat mountain bike tire adds a lot of impact absorbency.

SPOKED WHEELS
The vast majority of mountain bikes have spoked wheels. The wheel consists of a hub, spokes (usually 32 or 36) and an aluminum alloy rim. The spokes are laced into a wheel and the result is one of the greatest strength-to-weight structures available. Though early mountain bikes had extremely wide rims, modern mountain bikes typically have rims that are only around 1in (23mm) wide, under half the width of the tire used. This narrow rim gives a better balloon section, superior shock absorption, better traction and lighter weight. More expensive wheels use stronger, lighter rims; the rim surface may be treated with a high-friction ceramic coating, and the spokes are thinner and stronger, building a lighter wheel set.

RIMS
Rims are produced by forcing molten aluminum through a die. These long pieces of aluminum are then rolled into rims, pinned and joined and drilled with the holes required to take the spokes. Various surface treatments may be performed on the rim to improve its quality or appearance, including anodizing or ceramic coating.

HUBS

Mountain bike hubs are a standard size, with the hub being measured by its 'over-locknut dimension' – the distance between the locknuts at each end of the axle. For the rear hub this is $5\frac{1}{2}$in (135mm), and for the front hub it's 4in (100mm). Special-use suspension forks are instigating a new standard of $4\frac{1}{2}$in (110mm) diameter spacing at the front, with the axle clamping into place in the drop-out, rather than the drop-out being clamped between the axle and the quick-release skewer. The cassette of cogs runs on an integral freewheel mechanism located inside the hub, rather than the older-style self-contained freewheel units. This gives the rear hub the name 'freehub' and also provides better sealing of the freewheel bearings.

SPOKES

Although they look just like lengths of bent wire, a lot of technology goes into making a quality spoke. Mountain bike spokes are usually made from stainless steel and butted (that is, thinned in the middle, where stresses are the lowest). Titanium can be used as a spoke material, but it is typically 10 times more expensive than stainless steel!

COMPOSITE WHEELS

Spoked wheels are light, strong and good value, but manufacturers continue to promote the aerodynamic advantages of composite wheels. Made either from carbon fiber or blow-molded thermoplastic, these wheels are heavier, and sometimes weaker, than a spoked wheel, although they cut through the air better. This is an issue on road bikes (say, during a time trial), but for mountain bike use, they're not worth considering unless you're a sponsored rider.

TIRES

All modern mountain bikes use 26in tires. Some hybrid bikes run the road-bike 700C size, and GT played around with a 700D tire size a couple of years ago, but 26in is now king.

Tires are available in many widths, with the narrowest coming in at under 1in (2cm), and the widest hulking onto a rim at $2\frac{1}{2}$in (6cm), in cross-section. Tread profile, rubber type and casing construction can all vary, according to what the tire has to do. Some World Cup cross-country racers have taken to using almost slick-treaded tires, with pronounced knobs on the sides only. Downhillers use aggressively treaded, super-fat tires. Mud tires have a few widely spaced knobs. Tires are available with either a steel bead or a Kevlar bead. The supposed advantage of Kevlar tires is that they fold up – not much of an issue for mountain bikers, but the upshot is that the tire is lighter, which is good for racers. Some tires have anti-thorn strips under the tread and inner tubes are also available with impact pinch resistance.

ALTERNATIVE WHEELS
Composite wheels offer aerodynamic advantages that are of little consequence to a mountain biker, but they do look cool!

Suspension

The biggest development going on in mountain biking right now is suspension. Rock Shox were the first company to offer suspension forks to the mountain bike market, and now there are over a hundred different brands of forks, all competing for your money.

Most mountain bike forks are of the telescopic variety; a system similar to that used on a motor bike; an aluminum crown holds the steering tube and the stanchion tubes, all fixed firmly in place. The wheel is fitted into dropouts on the slider tubes, and as the fork is compressed, the stanchions compress into the sliders, compressing the spring. When the fork is released, it extends again, back to its normal ride-height.

The part that actually does the springing and controlling of the movement varies from one model to another. Some forks use elastomeric rubber bumpers that compress and rebound to control the movement. Others combine these elastomers with oil-filled cartridges to fine-tune the movement and improve the control of the fork. Downhill bikes, where weight is less critical, tend to use steel-sprung, oil-damped forks, for the best consistency.

LINKAGE FORKS

Other forks don't have the telescopic design, relying instead on parallelogram linkage design. The fork blades are fixed to the parallelogram, and, as the fork is compressed, the parallelogram compresses the spring medium. Of course, this is a battlefield in the hype wars. Telescopic fork designers say theirs is the right way; linkage designers say it has to be the other way around. At the time of writing, telescopic forks are more prevalent in the market, but that's all we can say. Good and bad examples of each abound.

REAR SUSPENSION

As speeds increased because front suspension systems were lessening the impact, riders soon realized that the same amount of travel at the back of the bike would be a very good thing. Clearly this isn't a bolt-on modification. Rear suspension systems are designed as part of a complete frame. Different manufacturers claim that their system is the best, and as suspension is only in its third or fourth year of development, there are all kinds of designs out there. Here are the leading ones.

MacPherson Strut

One of the first systems used was the MacPherson strut design, where the bike's chainstays are pivoted at the bottom bracket, and

linkage forks

telescopic front suspension

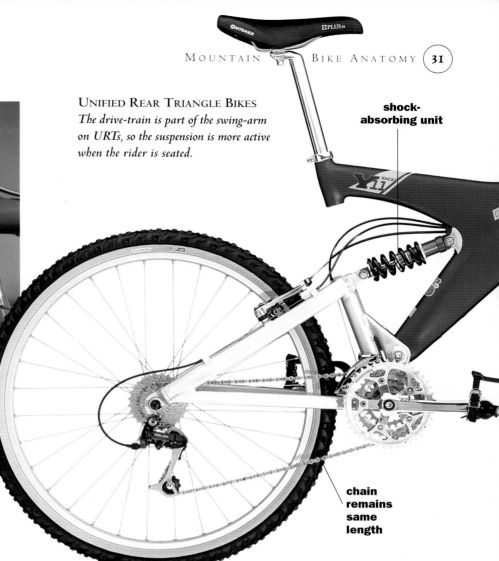

UNIFIED REAR TRIANGLE BIKES
The drive-train is part of the swing-arm on URTs, so the suspension is more active when the rider is seated.

shock-absorbing unit

chain remains same length

SPECIALIZED'S FSR SUSPENSION
Seen above is a typical example of the parallelogram rear suspension system.

a shock absorber is incorporated rigidly into the seatstays. Critical to the performance of many of these bikes is a 'Horst Link,' a design feature where the rear drop-outs are part of the seatstay assembly, rather than part of the chainstays. This produces a modified axle path, and a more constant chain length under load.

PARALLELOGRAM
First seen on Specialized's FSR bike, the parallelogram suspension system appears very much like the MacPherson design, until you get to the top of the seatstays. Instead of compressing a shock as part of the seatstays, this design pushes a link that compresses the shock unit. Its advantage is that the shock unit isn't stressed and doesn't affect the rigidity of the bike. The shock unit is simply left

with the job of absorbing shocks, rather than acting as a structural member – much more sensible.

ROCKER
The rocker bikes are a twist on regular parallelogram design. Here, instead of compressing the shock at the back of the bike, the shock is positioned in the main triangle, and squashed there. This lowers the bike's center of gravity slightly, but other than that produces little difference in performance.

UNIFIED REAR TRIANGLE
The suspension systems on many full-suspension bikes work so that, when the suspension is compressed,

the chain length of the bike changes. The URT design gives no such problems. Instead, the bottom bracket (along with the cranks, chainrings and all the rest of the drive-train) is part of the swinging arm, and moves with the rear suspension. Although this might sound strange, as long as the bottom bracket is close to the pivot point of the rear suspension, you hardly notice the movement of the bottom bracket. Some designs use pivot points further away from the bottom bracket, producing a bike that artificially locks itself out when you stand on the pedals, because the rear suspension is taking the rider's weight.

Steering and seating

The steering of your bike is where you'll first feel the trail shocks, so the right bars, stem and headset will all help you to get over those bumps. And a comfy seat can make more difference than you might have supposed.

RIDER CONTROL SET-UP
Bar, stem and headset choice are often as crucial to the front of a bike as the suspension fork.

BARS

Usually made of high-quality aluminum, standard mountain bike handlebars have a central diameter of 1in (25.4mm), and ends (where the grips and brake/shift levers attach) that measure ⅞in (22.2mm). Other materials are sometimes used for bars. Carbon fiber, thermoplastic, titanium, and even good old chromoly steel are all used in some bars, and all have certain advantages or disadvantages. Aluminum gives a good strength/weight/cost ratio, and is what most bikes come with.

Increasingly popular are 'riser' bars – bars with an upward bend that raises the position of the hand a couple of inches for a given stem size. These are popular with downhill riders, and also with riders who don't want an extreme, stretched-out position. For downhill use, the bars must have much thicker walls, and often come with a brace to strengthen the bar in its middle section.

chromoly stem

STEM AND HEADSET

The typical stem is made from welded chromoly or aluminum tube, and is available in lengths from 4 to 6in (100-150mm). Varying the stem offers the chance to customize the size of a bike, but, as a general rule, a long stem fitted to a small bike will result in too much weight on the front wheel, giving unpredictable (even potentially dangerous) steering.

Two standards of stem exist. The original standard for stems – 'quilled' units – clamped in place inside the steering tube with an expander-bolt fastening. The steering tube was threaded, and the headset could be adjusted by moving it on the threaded portion before being locked in place with a locknut. This sort of headset needs a large wrench (around 9in/23cm long) to adjust it. The cups that hold the bearings that the headset turns on are pressed into the frame.

The Aheadset system was introduced a couple of years ago, and uses a stem that clamps around the steering tube, like a stem clamping a handlebar. The headset is adjusted by sliding the stem up and down the steering tube, and when the stem is clamped in place, it locates everything firmly. This headset can be adjusted with one allen key. It still uses pressed-in cups, like a standard headset, but these only need to be changed when the headset is severely worn.

A few manufacturers have introduced radically different headsets (notably Klien), but by and large, the 1.125in Aheadset unit is standard across most quality bikes.

BAR ENDS

Clamping on the ends of the handlebar, bar ends allow another more aerodynamic position for the mountain biker. They also give a powerful position when climbing out of the saddle, though they're really only useful on smooth trails. Riding bumpy trails while using the bar ends is hazardous due to the decreased control they give.

BAR ENDS

Having an alternative riding position means you can put more power into your pedal strokes.

GRIPS

The handlebars have rubber or foam grips on the ends, to act as a protective barrier against bumping and jarring. Many, many different designs of grip are available, in a vast array of colors! If you have small hands, it makes sense to fit small grips. Cheaper bikes may have foam grips fitted that seem comfy at first, but then actually make the hands ache more than bare metal would. Change your grips if

you're not happy with them, and try as many as you can before you decide on a set.

SADDLE

Mountain bike saddles don't differ much from those on other sorts of bikes. The usual differences are slightly more padding, and a design that's tougher and more capable of standing up to the knocks that saddles get when you ride – or crash! – off-road. Kevlar protective bumpers, toughened cases and small, shock-absorbing mounts are par for the course.

SEATPOST

Clamping into the seat-tube, the seatpost supports the saddle, and also allows it to be angled or moved forward and backward, in order to get it into the comfiest position for the rider. Mountain bike seatposts are longer than those on road bikes, as mountain bike frames are smaller. A smaller frame means that the top tube of the bike is lower, so that, when you have to leap off on a tricky maneuver, you won't hurt yourself by crashing into the top tube. All that's important on a mountain bike is the relative positions of the saddle, bars and pedals. There's nothing wrong with using a super-long seatpost on a small frame, providing that the post and the frame are strong enough to take it, and that the frame is long enough (from bars to saddle) for you to ride without feeling cramped.

CHAPTER TWO

Getting started

*So you want to buy a mountain bike?
Mountain bikes have to be much stronger than
other types of bike because they suffer more
abuse on the trail. That's also why they cost
more than traditional sorts of bicycle — not
only do they have to be strong enough to
withstand the stresses, but they also shouldn't
be unreasonably heavy. These are the basic
facts, but there are many types of bike —
reading this chapter will guide you
through the minefield of choices.*

Buying a mountain bike

The most important thing to ensure when buying a mountain bike is that it's the right size. Buy a bike that's too small, and you'll have to find a long seat post which, if you're heavy, will place a lot of stress on the post.

Cheap mountain bikes weighing in at 35lb (16kg) or more aren't uncommon. Suspension forks and rear suspension systems add to a bike's weight of course, but a regular, rigid bike for off-road riding should weigh in at around the 25lb (11kg) mark.

Cheap bikes weigh more because they're made from cheaper, weaker materials, used in greater quantities to build a bike that's strong enough to ride off-road.

Of course, not everyone can afford to spend as much as they'd like on whatever they want – most people have to work within a budget. However, remember that, even if you spend a lot, mountain bikes are far from bomb-proof – you'd be dreaming if you thought you could ride a bike week-in, week-out without problems.

THE RIGHT SIZE FRAME
The key factor is standover height. You should have at least 3in (8cm) – the width of your palm – between the top of the top tube, and the top of your legs, when you're standing with your feet flat on the floor.

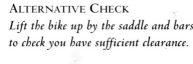

allow at least 3in (8cm) clearance above top tube

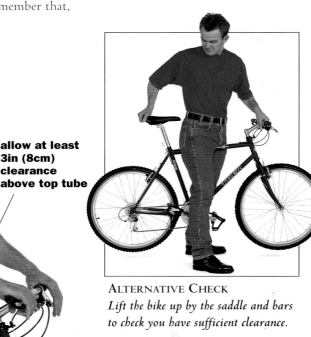

ALTERNATIVE CHECK
Lift the bike up by the saddle and bars to check you have sufficient clearance.

BUYING ON A BUDGET

When on a budget, the best advice is to buy a completely standard, sensibly equipped, steel-framed bike, without a suspension fork. This is what most mountain bikers were riding around on before suspension started taking over the market, and it's more than good enough to cover any trails that anyone else rides. Buying a bike without a suspension fork (and without rear suspension, fancy frame materials or other things that raise the cost of the bike) means that, for a given price, you're getting better components on the bike. Better components means

that hubs are better sealed, cranks are stronger, and everything will work for longer and more efficiently, with fewer problems.

Make sure your bike comes with good metal pedals (not cheap plastic ones) and toeclips, and consider a set of bar ends at the time of purchase – you should be able to haggle yourself a pair.

SECOND-HAND

Another option for getting into mountain biking is to go for a second-hand bike, but this area is a minefield of potential disasters as you've no idea of the history of the bike you're getting. Never, ever, buy a second-hand bike without getting it inspected by a friend who knows about mountain biking

CORRECT SET-UP
A good cycling store will help you to tune your bike so that it fits you and your needs perfectly.

relaxed shoulders

slight bend in arms

body not over-stretched

leg should be almost straight

mechanics. Things like frame damage are easy to spot if you're looking for it; miss it, however, and you could have the front half of your bike separate from the rest of it. The best bike to buy will be a year or two old and barely used, perhaps only on roads. Take a look at any owner's current bike and see what it's like to get an idea about how they look after their pride and joy. Beware!

MORE MONEY = MORE BIKE

Once you've crossed the bargain threshold, then, quite simply, the more money you spend, the better quality you get. As already explained, a steel frame with a rigid fork is the cheapest option, although this type of bike is available throughout the price lines. The more you pay, the better the quality of the steel used in the frame and the better the quality of the components; as a result, the whole bike will also be lighter.

Suspension forks and more exotic frame materials will always add to the price of rigid steel-framed bikes. Full suspension typically adds to the price of a mountain bike – and also adds 2-41b (1-2kg) in weight.

Specialization – for downhill and cross-country – brings even higher prices. Racing tends to (mis) guide the design of bikes, to the point where it's difficult to find a high-priced bike for other purposes, such as off-road touring. Thankfully, custom builders still exist who can make a machine capable of anything. Or you could do worse than swapping low-slung race stems for higher rise, comfort-position ones.

Upgrading your bike

Once you've got your bike, there's no problem with changing parts to suit your riding style. Unlike cars, where one manufacturer's parts won't fit another's, bicycle frames are all built pretty much to the same standard.

There are a couple of areas where you can go wrong, but, by and large, the majority of parts can be swapped freely between bikes. However, where you've got a manufacturer's dedicated system (say a hub that takes a specific set of sprockets), you can get into trouble. Cranks must match up with bottom brackets of a specific length, or the chainrings will catch on the frame. There are even a couple of different standards of chainring that must fit on their specific crank. Brakes fit on a standard pivot, but with V brakes, you must use V brake compatible brake levers to operate them.

However, the long and short of it is that, it is possible to fit new components that aren't exactly the same as those on your bike. Take your derailleurs, for example. All Shimano units have the same geometry, but the more expensive models are better-made, better-sealed and will last for longer, so there's no problem with upgrading derailleurs to a more expensive model if funds allow it.

SADDLE
Saddles are far better than they used to be, but if you're still suffering discomfort after a few rides, then consider a change. Wearing proper cycling shorts can also help, as can altering the angle of the saddle on the seat post, but it might just be that your saddle is the wrong shape for you. There are many different designs — heavily padded, firm, sprung, Kevlar reinforced, super-lightweight, extra long... Have a go on a few people's bikes and consult your local dealer.

THE FIVE BEST UPGRADES

DERAILLEUR CABLING

Mountain bike derailleur systems run remarkably well, considering the abuse they suffer. Despite running them in a combination of mud, grit and rainwater, we expect them to work in all situations, faultlessly. Upgrading your derailleur cables by swapping them for a fully-sealed system, such as Goretex's cable set-ups, or using a cable-assister like a Cog Hog or a Roll-a-majig — means that your derailleurs work better, for longer. Which means that you can spend more time riding.

SUSPENSION FORKS

If your bike has a rigid fork, and the riding that you do means you're getting bashed about a lot, adding a suspension fork to your bike is a good move. However, adding a suspension fork to a really cheap bike isn't a good move. That bike will be heavy already, and adding a fork, invariably a cheap one if you've a limited budget, will mean that it's heavier still. Suspension forks make sense for more expensive bikes, as long as you add a good-quality fork.

TERRAIN-SPECIFIC TIRES

The tires that your bike comes with are usually of an off-road capable design, which the manufacturer happened to get a good deal on. If you're riding on lots of different sorts of terrain, then a general use tire will work OK, but if the tracks you ride on are more specific (very muddy, dry, smooth, loose or whatever), then you'll benefit from changing tires to something that copes well in that situation. Consult your local store for what works well in your area. Trying to ride a mud tire on hardpacked tracks (or the other way round) can make a big difference to how well your bike performs.

CLIPLESS PEDALS

One of the best upgrades that anyone can make to a mountain bike is to invest in a set of clipless pedals and dedicated cycling shoes. Proper cycling shoes have a stiff sole that doesn't flex when you're pedaling, so that all the energy from your leg-action goes into driving the bike forward, not sliding your shoes about on the pedals. Clipless pedals use a click-in, twist-out latch action, which means that you're securely fixed to your pedals when you want to be, but you can release the pedal to get a foot down if you have to.

Trail bikes

If you're after a regular bike to ride around on regular trails, then this is for you. The key features on a trail bike are good front suspension and a sensible choice of components.

The 'regular' mountain bike – the sort of thing that most riders either have or aspire to own – will have a frame built from high-quality steel, aluminum or carbon. With a well-balanced suspension fork, this bike will give trouble-free service for years. Trail riding doesn't take lack of weight as its primary cue, and so a frame for a competent trail bike should be as strong as it is light. Erring too far to the weight-shaving side of things isn't a good idea, although it doesn't mean that trail bikes can't be light. Super-light steel and aluminum bikes, however, are more at home on the race track, rather than under a super-hard trail rider.

WHEELS AND TIRES

It can't be stressed enough that superlight wheel assemblies are fine for racing, but when a wheel failure could mean a long walk home, it's best to look for wheels that can offer reliability. Tires should also be suitable for the country that you're going to be crossing. If the trails around you vary in their condition at different times of the year, then get yourself several sets of tires, and switch them according to the trail conditions at the time you're riding.

RIDING POSITION

If you're going to be spending a lot of time on the trail, it's best to be comfortable. A good saddle and comfortable handlebar grips are only half the story, as you should be comfortable on the bike as well. A stem that's too low will strain your back over time, but one that places you too upright will jarr your spine, and won't give a biomechanically efficient position for the climbs. Don't be afraid to change the stem or bar for a shorter or higher-reach model, as comfort on long rides is important. You're meant to be enjoying yourself!

FORK

Suspension is a new addition to mountain biking. It's not essential, as it's primarily a comfort thing, but the comfort that it gives you allows you to ride for longer without getting as tired. It'll ease the bumping on downhills, and let you go quite a bit faster, too. Suspension forks may take some getting used to if you've ridden rigid forks, because body movement can cause them to compress which, while not making you lose energy, nevertheless feels a bit strange. Over time, having suspension feels far more normal, and you can use it to its best advantage.

SADDLE

When you're going to be spending a lot of time out on the trail, ensure that your saddle is comfortable. The type of clothing you wear (get some cycling shorts) and the angle of your saddle (move it on the seat post) can affect the comfort, but make sure that the saddle itself is right for you. Quality costs, so buy the best you can – you'll really feel the difference.

CLIPLESS PEDALS

Although you might not be convinced that these mechanical-action pedals will actually work in the muddy and rock-strewn environment of off-road riding, you'd be totally wrong. They're tough and reliable, and make riding a bike through rough ground much easier, as your feet stay firmly fixed to the pedals, with no worrying about slipping off and losing control.

shortish reach stem

good standover height

PRIVATEER COMP

BONTRAGER

telescopic suspension forks

clipless pedals

choose tires to suit the conditions

> ### OTHER ACCESSORIES
> *The various components that are available are aimed at making a trail-rider self-sufficient. Despite the advances in technology, the humble flat tire is still a problem that can halt even the most expensive bike. Trail riders should carry a pump, tools and a spare tube to ensure that they're not stopped by mechanical breakdown. A simple fender is also a good idea for wet climates, providing that they can be used without problems such as the fenders flapping into the tires.*

Full-suspension bikes

Suspension is often seen as a downhill-only technology, but if you can have a bike that's light, reliable and comfortable, then why not ride it all the time? Modern full suspension bikes are just that, and they mean that you can spend a day in the saddle without feeling like you've gone eighteen rounds with a heavyweight.

Quite simply, a full-suspension, lightweight trail bike is the comfiest thing to spend time on if the terrain is even moderately bumpy. And once again – full suspension doesn't have to mean downhill. Downhill parts are designed for the even greater stresses involved in the crash-and-bash of racing, and can result in bikes weighing about 10lb (4-5kg) more than cross-country models. A full-suspension bike weighs more than a rigid bike already, so don't pile on overweight, unsuitable parts if you're riding regular trails.

REAR SHOCK
Tuning the rear shock of a full-suspension bike is a job that should really be done by the designers. You'll find, however, that the damping settings on some bikes, especially early full-suspension models, make them harsh when going over bumps. This is the result of too much

OTHER ACCESSORIES
If you're trail-riding, then take the trail accessories listed in the previous bike's specification. The usual stuff – tools, tubes, pumps, fenders (if you need them), but keep it light. Riding a heavy, full-suspension bike is no fun. Riding a light one is the business!

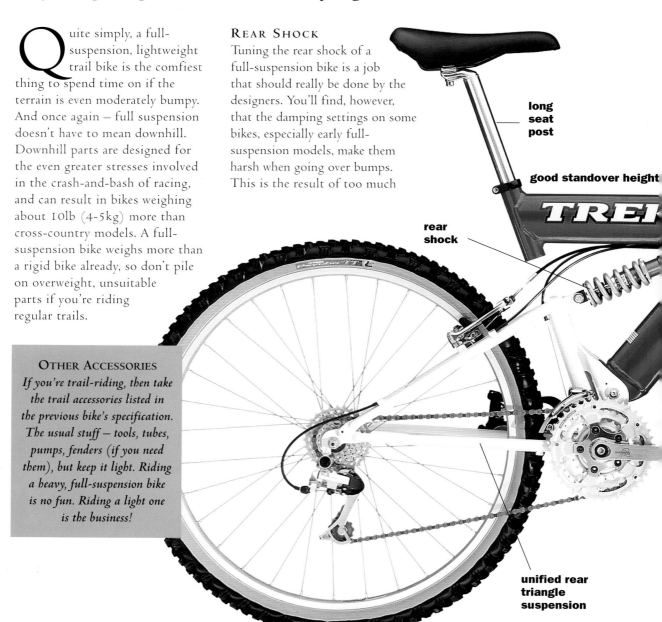

long
seat
post

good standover height

rear
shock

unified rear
triangle
suspension

damping, to minimize any potential bobbing under the pedal load. Learning to ride more smoothly, throwing your weight about less, means that a lighter damping setting can be used, making the suspension actually do its job.

LIGHTWEIGHT WHEELS
Although a suspension bike is inevitably going to cost more than a rigid bike, don't skimp on the wheel set. Wheels that are heavy don't accelerate as well as a light set – indeed, one particular old cycling saying states that 'an ounce off the wheels is worth a pound off the frame.' It's not quite that severe, but checking that the rims, hubs and spokes are a good weight, and also fitting lightweight tires and inner tubes, will usually ensure that your mountain bike doesn't sprint or climb badly.

SUSPENSION FORK
A fully functioning suspension bike has to have more than just a shock at each end; the rates of the shocks should be tuned so that they work well together. Set up wrongly, the bike will buck about through bumpy sections. It's not essential to have the same sort of suspension at each end of the bike, but it is important to make sure that they compress at the same rate.

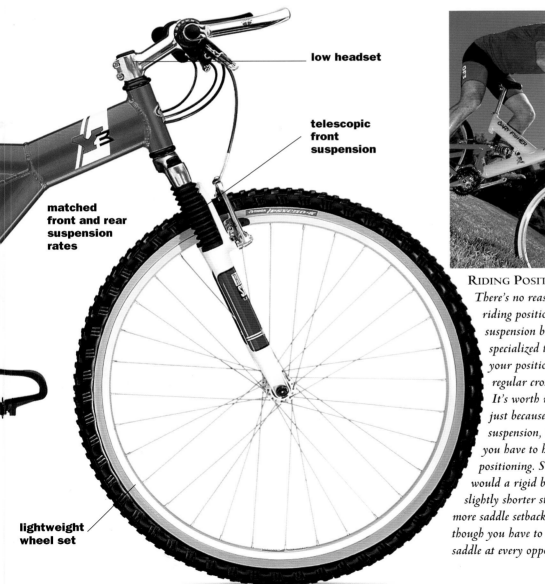

low headset

telescopic front suspension

matched front and rear suspension rates

lightweight wheel set

RIDING POSITION
There's no reason to change your riding position on a full-suspension bike, but, the more specialized the use, the more your position will differ from a regular cross-country stance. It's worth remembering that, just because a bike has full suspension, it doesn't mean that you have to have downhill positioning. Set it up as you would a rigid bike, but with a slightly shorter stem and a little more saddle setback, so you don't feel as though you have to climb out of the saddle at every opportunity.

Cross-country racers

The bikes that the pros ride differ even from the stock, high-end bikes that are available in the stores. Pro riders pick and choose equipment to suit themselves, and put up with large amounts of discomfort to save a little weight or get a more efficient pedaling position. Narrow tires, narrow bars and hard saddles are just some of the ways they try to extract more speed.

Racing frame sets are single-minded in their approach. They're designed to go uphill as fast as possible, even if that compromises their performance on the downs and bumps somewhat. Pro-level race bikes are light – under 23lb (10.5kg), even with a suspension fork. They're built around the lightest frames possible; there have been cases of super-light frames being built for specific races, and then retired.

COMPONENTS

Weight is the issue here, with strength a consideration. Over-built components shouldn't be fitted to race bikes, but parts that skimp on strength in vital areas have no place either – 'to finish first, first you've got to finish!'. Tire sizes are usually as narrow as possible, and there is an increase in the number of riders using semi-slick tires (almost treadless in the center, with knobs at the sides for cornering). These tires are light, fast and for pro use only.

HANDLEBARS

While many riders would be uncomfortable with a low position, off-road racers use narrow, low handlebars. This puts them in a powerful position, with their body weight well over their

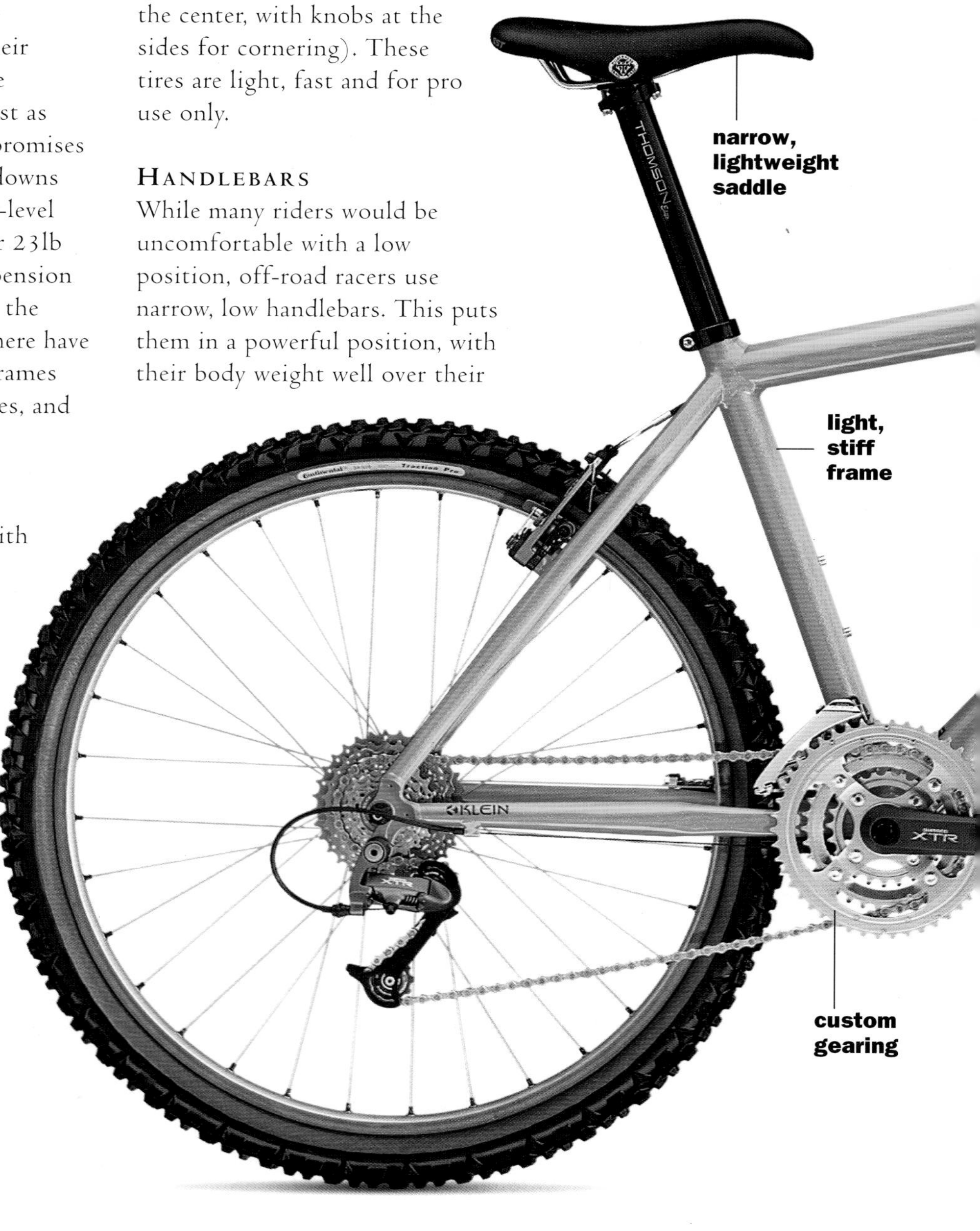

narrow, lightweight saddle

light, stiff frame

custom gearing

legs, giving them extra leverage. It's more aerodynamic, too. It does compromise descending stability, where too much weight on the front wheel isn't a good thing, but then, cross-country races are usually won on the climbs, rarely on the descents.

TIRES

Narrower than you'd probably choose, racing mountain bike tires are undergoing development at the moment. Faster courses are inspiring semi-slick designs with minimal tread on their centers, and the only pronounced knobs are at the sides, to grip on the corners. Pros that don't use these generally run 1.5in (4cm) tires, pumped to a high pressure on all but the rockiest courses, where they'll choose 1.9in (5cm) rubber.

GEARING

There's a lot of standardization in component groups, but many pro-level riders will mix and match their gearing — even changing the set-up to suit specific races. If a race has a particularly steep climb, or lots of flat, fast tracks, then riders will pick their front chainrings accordingly, to gain an advantage over other racers.

RIDING POSITION

As most of the training for off-road racing is done on the road (because training can be monitored much more closely), many mountain bike racers adopt a position that's a bit longer than would be comfortable for a trail rider. This gets the rider into a more aerodynamic position, which isn't strictly necessary for mountain bike racing, but is always helpful. Also, ensuring that the bike is as close to a road position as possible means that the stresses on the muscles are almost identical.

super-light wheels and lightweight tires

clipless pedals

OTHER ACCESSORIES
Mountain bike racing is a self-sufficient sport — racers have to fix any problems themselves. A basic racing fix-it kit includes a spare tube, CO2 inflators, tire levers, chain tool and a couple of allen keys. If anything more complex breaks, most competitors will simply retire.

Downhill bikes

Downhill bikes are now much, much more than simply a regular frame with a set of suspension forks added on. Downhilling has turned into the cutting edge of mountain bike technology.

Until recently, riders were competing in downhills on bikes that were the same as those on the cross-country circuit, except for the addition of some two-inch travel suspension forks. Now, most downhill riders are riding full-suspension bikes, with at least six inches of travel at each end, which weigh 10-15lb (20-30kg) more than a cross-country bike. Frames must be super-strong. The forces that a dual-crown fork can put through a frame can rip the front off a regular bike, so something that's gussetted, even a totally box-section frame, makes sense. Forget weight; its strength that matters.

COMPONENTS

Brakes and chain devices are two of the most important parts of a downhill bike. Many competitors are using disc brakes, giving superior stopping power over the more established cantilevers or V brakes. Chain devices are used to keep the chain on the single chain ring that downhill bikes run. A chain dropping off can make the difference between finishing and crashing out.

DOUBLE CROWN FORKS

Downhill bikes are getting to look more and more like motorbikes without engines. The suspension forks they use are now specifically designed for downhill use, with the stanchion tubes extended to

reinforced frame

OTHER ACCESSORIES
Tires are far bigger than on regular cross-country bikes, to give better traction on changeable surfaces. Some form of flat resistance will usually be used.

the top of the headtube, where they're clamped with another crown. This holds everything securely in place, and provides a better steering response.

REINFORCED FRAME

The forces that double-crown forks can exert on a bike frame are huge – far larger than regular forks

– and so frames must be built stronger. That means not only using thicker-than-usual tubing, but also reinforcing that tubing with gussets and plates to add further strength. Even then, frames will rarely last more than half a season under the hardest downhillers.

PEDALS

Downhill riders used to be torn between the security of clipless pedals, and the freedom of movement of spiked, flat pedals. Now, thanks to Shimano's new DX SPD pedal, they've got the best of both worlds. Riders can clip into the pedal or rest on the spiked cage of the flat pedal and be able to get a foot down when they need to.

RIDING POSITION

Downhill bikes are set up with a shorter, higher riding position, so that the bike's easier to control. Stems are higher, and put the bars closer to the rider. This lessens the weight on the front wheel, which can result in a laid-back feeling on the flat. Bars aren't typically straight ones, but swept back and angled upwards to give a high position. Point this sort of bike downhill, though, and it all works much better. This means setting up the suspension forks quite hard and the rear shock soft, so that, when the weight's on the front wheel, everything still works properly.

'riser' bars (high-rise handlebars)

double crown forks

flat pedals

disc brake

large tires

Trials bikes

If you're going to hop and jump your bike over obstacles, then you'll need something very different. You'll find that trials bikes are pretty useless for riding around mountainsides, but great for riding over logs and blocks!

Just as downhill bikes no longer bear much resemblance to those used in cross-country race competition, so trials bikes bear little relation to anything else labelled 'mountain bike'. Frames are super-strong and low, to allow the rider room to move around on the bike. Aluminum is the most common material for trials bikes, mainly because of its strength and rigidity, and also because many trials-bike manufacturers come from a motorcycle background.

COMPONENTS

Trials bikes don't need many gears, suspension or a comfortable riding position. The things that matter are grippy tires and pedals, and good brakes. The tires need to be able to hold traction on many different sorts of surface (wood, plastic, glass, dirt), while the pedals must have a dog-like-grip on the shoes. The brakes have to be capable of locking a wheel with light hand-pressure.

low saddle

OTHER ACCESSORIES
Some trials bikes have gears, to enable a rider to move quickly between trials obstacles, but they're not essential. A bash guard, built into the frame, is another useful component dedicated for trials use.

FRONT SUSPENSION

When you're landing off large platforms, rocks or whatever, then it's good to have something to take the sting out of the landing. Suspension forks, set up stiffly so as not to affect the handling too much, are useful for the adventurous trials user.

'riser' bars

RIMS

Trials riders use wide rims, with the braking surfaces covered in something sticky. The width of the rim is to provide strength, and to support a wide tire. The sticky rim sidewalls are to aid braking, and the sticky substance used varies from place to place. In the UK, riders use road tar. In the US, Coke has been known to be used.

BRAKES

If you can't lock the wheels, then you can't do trials. Pro-level trials require the rider to be able to hop the bike around. In order to make any progress, the wheels mustn't spin, or you'll lose traction. Magura hydraulic brakes are the commonest in use.

RIDING POSITION

Trials bikes aren't really ridden. They're hopped, jumped, twisted and clambered — onto logs, blocks, pallets and cars. The riding position is all about the relationship between the pedals and the handlebars. The upswept bars are clamped in a stem that raises them well above a regular bike's position, and close to that of a downhill bike.

flat pedals

alternative – Magura hydraulic brakes

Multi-track bike

If you're not inclined to attack the 'mountain' aspect of mountain biking, then a different style of bike might suit you better. Using larger-diameter wheels, but with mountain bike components, the multi-track bike is the commuter's choice.

For riding around cities and off-roading, a multi-track bike still requires a suitably tough frame, though it doesn't have to be up to the strength of a true off-road bike. Paintwork should be tough, to protect against nicks and scrapes, and the frame should have fixings for fenders, and possibly a rack. Most multi-track bikes are made from steel of a reasonable (though not excellent) quality. That's not to say that aluminum isn't suitable, but steel is the material of choice.

COMPONENTS

The gearing on a multi-track bike, though obviously specific to the terrain that it's going to be ridden over, can be higher than that found on an off-road bike. This is noticeably achieved by multi-track bikes that have 700C wheels fitted, rather than the smaller 26in wheels fitted to mountain bikes. Additionally, some bikes may come fitted with a road-pattern double chainset, rather than an off-road standard triple unit.

RACK

There's no point in carrying everything in a backpack when you can slam things in a bag mounted to your rack. Cheap

long seat post

pump

pannier racks

fenders

road tires

chainguard

OTHER ACCESSORIES

A rack and fenders are extremely useful fittings. Riders are less likely to want to 'rough it,' and are more interested in using the bike to get about on. Lights are also essential if the bike's to be used as a commuting vehicle.

panniers are ideal, and some companies even make briefcases that unzip from their mountings to allow you to carry them on their own. Racks are also the best place to carry a U-lock — essential for bike security.

HIGH STEM

Though it's not considered 'cool,' sitting up high and being able to see properly is a real benefit for the commuting rider. You are more aware of the traffic around you, and can be prepared for when a car cuts through traffic and into your path.

FENDERS

Riding in regular clothes, rather than cycling clothes, you'll want to keep yourself dry, so fenders are essential for all except the driest climates. If you're riding hard, then it's best to wear proper cycling clothes, but even then, limiting the spray from the road isn't a bad thing.

RIDING POSITION

Off-road bikes have a high bottom bracket, typically about 12in (30cm) off the ground. Because there are less obstacles to ride over on paved surfaces, the bottom bracket of a multi-track bike will be about 1in (2cm) lower. This will mean that there's less of a climb to the saddle, so that getting on the bike is easier. Other design pointers help to create a riding position that's more upright than other bikes, making looking around and checking the traffic out much easier.

lights

water bottle holder

Touring bikes

Mountain bikes make the ideal traveling companion for rough roads and foreign terrain. Many people, even inexperienced cyclists, use mountain bikes as their way of seeing the world. There are several things to consider when choosing or tuning a bike for a trip.

Steel is the material of choice for the traveler, because, in any small settlement, anywhere in the world, there'll be someone who can weld or braze a steel frame back together — as long as it's not made from very thin-walled tubing. As attractive and robust as aluminum, carbon fiber or titanium frames may appear to be, the same claim can't be made.

COMPONENTS

If possible, pick simple, solid components that are tough and durable. Excessively lightweight parts have no place on a bike that's going to be weighed down with luggage and ridden long and hard. Run-of-the-mill regular groups from Shimano will work fine. Finely-tuned exotica might be too fragile.

WHEELS

Choose your wheels with care. If you can't afford custom-built wheelsets before a trip, take your existing wheels to a good store for an overhaul. Tell them what you're going to do, and have the wheels completely overhauled, the spokes checked, and new tires and tubes fitted. If you're off on a long trip, there's no point in taking half worn-out equipment.

light

saddle-pack

panniers

reflector

fender

OTHER ACCESSORIES
Aside from the obvious racks, panniers and other carrying equipment, make sure that the wheels and tires you choose are up to the job. Carrying folding tires is a good idea, as a ripped tire means you can't ride, however well the rest of your bike is working.

SADDLE

Going to be spending a long time in the saddle? Get a saddle you're comfortable with and ride it for some time before you leave. Don't use the trip as an opportunity to try out new positions and equipment; you might not like it, and you might be very uncomfortable.

RACKS

Don't skimp on the racks. If you're going to be carrying heavy equipment, cheaply made aluminum racks will snap or bend in no time. Some of the best around come from Blackburn. Like all things, you get what you pay for. As a rule, try to spend a little more than you can afford.

RIDING POSITION

Long days in the saddle call for a bike that's really comfortable. Adding bar ends will not only give you a more aerodynamic position for cycling in headwinds, but it'll also allow you a change of position — very welcome after six hours in the saddle.

water bottles

slick tires

toeclips

fender

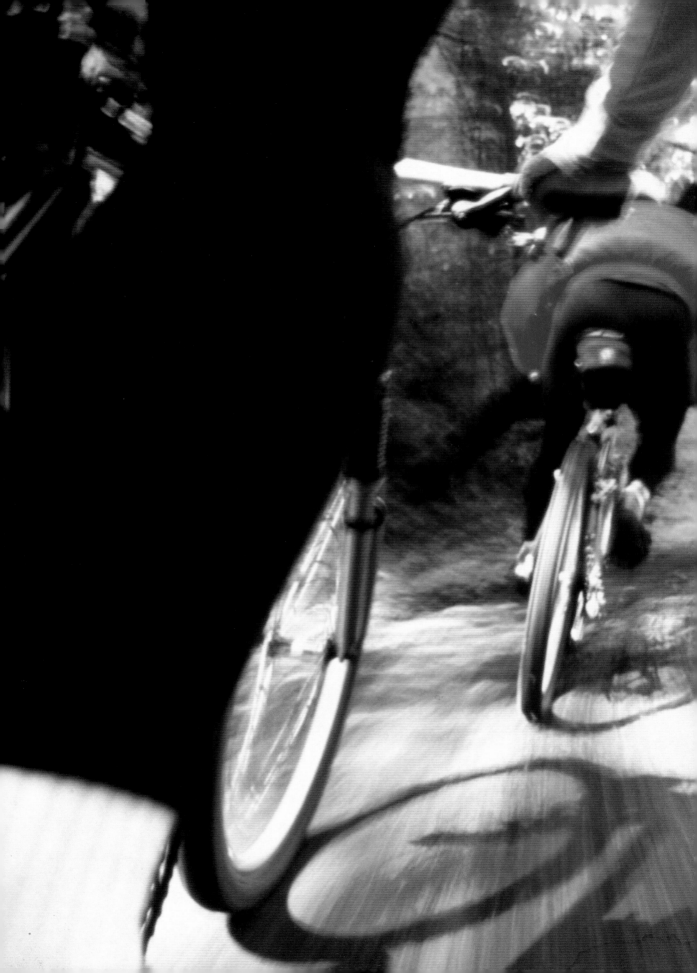

CHAPTER THREE

Trail-ready

The first thing you'll find out about mountain biking is that it pays to be well prepared. Safety, comfort, route planning, general maintenance and a basic knowledge of trailside repairs are all prerequisites for the average 'trail warrior'. In this chapter, we'll be looking in detail at what you'll need to know in order to make your off-road experiences more fulfilling.

Dressing for safety and comfort

There's little point in having a great bike if your clothing isn't remotely suitable. You don't need to spend a fortune on all the latest fads, but certain items will make all the difference.

CLOSE-FITTING COMFORT
More than the rest of the cycling world, mountain biking takes its clothing cues from the world of outdoor pursuits. Comfort and a sleek, close fit are the major keys.

COLD-WEATHER WEAR
Outdoor world garments such as fleeces are ideal for cooler weather. Fleeces come in different weights — a lightweight one is shown here — and so can be layered.

As disposable incomes have risen, cycling kit has become as much fashion- as function led. New materials and inspired designs have provided a wide range of top-quality clothing, helmets, shoes, glasses and gloves. Even low-cost cycling kit offers greater comfort and a better image than at any other time, and it's all much more practical than sawn-off jeans, teeshirts and jogging shoes.

You will hear riders talking about the 'technical' properties of their clothing, referring to features like thermal ratings, cooling properties, breathability and air flow. Some of this is simply successful marketing spiel that'll make only tiny differences to your overall ride experience, but it's still worth taking a look at any advances that are likely to concern you.

SHORTS

Cycling shorts range from tight Lycra with padded inserts to casual baggies with all the seams in the right places. For distance riding, the most comfy shorts are multi-panel ones in Lycra-mix materials, with single-piece anti-bacterial inserts, especially those in the bib style, but not everyone likes the image of Lycra. Many clothing companies are now making baggy shorts with a close-fitting, padded inner short, so you get the non-Lycra image and the practicality all in one.

LONGS

Cycling longs are best in a Lycra mix, worn either over shorts or under baggies. You can wear thermal mixes for winter conditions, or you can even get leg-warmers to pull on and off on changeable days. Wool is also making a small comeback, in leg-warmers, shorts and jerseys.

JERSEYS

Jersey material and styles vary enormously, from the multicolored, sponsorship-emblazoned Lycra of race teams to plain primary colors in cotton, wool and polyester mixes. Choose long- or short-sleeved in different materials for different seasons. Some of the long-sleeved winter jerseys are like mid-weight fleeces. You can add arm-warmers to short sleeves in changeable weather.

VESTS

There are two types of cycling vest; base layer and top layer. A base-layer vest should be made of a

WARM WEATHER WEAR

High-quality wicking fabrics — drawing sweat away from the body — are used to keep the cyclist cool as temperatures climb.

'wicking', quick-drying material like Polartech or one of the many polypropylene mixes. Top-layer vests can take the form of sleeveless windproofs or fleeces.

JACKETS

There's a massive range of cycling-specific top layers these days, from heavy-duty waterproofs to shower tops that scrunch down into tiny packs and fleeces of various densities and character. The main things to look for in a cycling jacket are long arms to accommodate your stretch on the bike and a long back to protect you from rear wheel spray. Map and food pockets are also very useful and breathability is more crucial than with any other layer. Breathability can be achieved through the use of technical fabrics or lots of zips.

WET-WEATHER WEAR
Don't skimp on this – the better trade names usually do offer a better-quality product and there's nothing worse than being wet on the trail.

URBAN ATTIRE
A face mask is considered essential by many city cyclists, but be prepared for feeling hot and sweaty.

GLOVES

At all times of the year, gloves of some sort are almost an essential for comfortable riding. Fingerless gloves will protect your hands from the vibration of the trail and potential damage when falling. They'll also improve your grip when your hands are sweaty or muddy. If you buy proper cycling gloves, they will have all the reinforcements and padding in the right places. If you buy leather gloves, make sure they're easy to wash; gloves can get dirty off-road.

GLASSES

You'll find that wearing glasses off-road will keep all the dirt out of your eyes. Some riders however, are not so keen – they complain that the build-up of sweat on the inside of the lenses makes glasses difficult to wear in extreme riding situations.

SHOES

Cycling shoes range from the totally casual touring or boot styles to serious race shoes covered with studs and straps. The one thing they all have in common is a stiffer sole than most other shoes. If you ride in ordinary shoes, you'll soon find that the pedals start to dig into the sole. When buying cycle shoes, get some with a covered recess for clipless cleats; if you don't use them now, you might in the future.

CHOOSING A HELMET

A helmet should be your first purchase. In some countries, wearing a helmet when cycling is compulsory. But even if it isn't, it's always advisable. Crashing is an integral part of learning to ride off-road, and you will never stop learning because pushing the boundaries is simply a part of the mountain biking experience. Every store offers a big range of helmets. The main thing to get right is the fit. If helmets don't fit properly, they will slip as soon as you fall, leaving part of your head vulnerable. Spend time trying on different models; we all have differently shaped heads. The padding that comes with helmets is for fine-tuning only; make sure the basic shape of the helmet is a good fit before you stuff in extra padding. Always check that a helmet conforms to safety standards set by institutes like Snell or ANSI (in the USA), Eu (Europe), BSI (UK) or AS (Australia); this will be marked inside the helmet. The more you pay for a helmet, the more features it will have. The coolest helmets, in both temperature and image terms, are, predictably, often the most costly.

BRIGHT COLORS AND BILLS
Bright colors are a sensible safety measure; while bills keep both the sun and rain out of your eyes.

GETTING THE RIGHT FIT
Make sure that your helmet is fitting perfectly, with the straps positioned as shown. A loose helmet will slip on impact, exposing your head to damage.

Fixtures and fittings

Once you've got your bike, and probably while you're getting it, you'll become aware of the vast range of MTB paraphernalia that people keep insisting you must acquire. Some of it is pretty much essential to any rider. Other stuff comes under a 'luxury' heading. You'll acquire it over the years as you need it.

Get all this stuff while you're buying the bike. If you don't, you'll be begging, stealing and borrowing it from irritated ride partners. The guiding light of mountain biking is self-sufficiency.

PUMP

For pumping efficiency, the frame-fitting type is better, but beware of the cheapest ones on the market, which tend to leak, bend or explode at crucial times. Mini pumps are popular among mountain bikers because they're light in weight and easy to carry in a small pack; many of them come with frame attachment clips. Again, beware of the cheap ones; even the best ones take a while to inflate a tire, the worst just won't do the job properly.

LIGHTS

Think carefully about what sort of lights you need. If you do a lot of night riding, you'll need to spend a fair amount of money on an up-market system that allows you to see trails clearly and to stay safe

and legal on roads leading to and from the trail. Even if you're not really a night rider, it's useful to have front and rear 'emergency' lights for those occasions where you get caught off guard by evenings closing in. Small, flashing lights are not street-legal in all countries, but they're easy to keep in your trail pack and they're far safer than nothing at all.

WATER BOTTLE

If you're planning to ride for more than about half an hour, fit at least one water bottle and cage; most MTBs come equipped for two. Many cyclists drink too little liquid, resulting in dehydration and its debilitating effects. Other water-carrying systems, like the Camelback, are popular, particularly among those who ride for more than a couple of

hours. Some Camelback-type packs come with pouches for food and accessories.

TOOL PACK

There are many ways of carrying tools, food, spares and extra clothing. Pockets are good enough for the lighter weight stuff, but most riders will use some sort of pack system. You can choose anything from the total solution – a backpack with a water-bladder sleeve – to a fanny pack or under-saddle pack. Most cycling-specific packs come with a useful array of pockets and straps – and possibly a mini-pump sleeve. Your pack should always contain at least:

1 a spare tube
2 a patch kit
3 tire levers
4 a spoke key
5 a spare chainlink
6 **tools for minor trail repairs**

There are a variety of multi-tools available which also include a device for splitting chain links.

THE LUXURY COLLECTION

You may not need this stuff, but it will make life easier as you progress from beginner to trail warrior. We've covered some of this in further detail in the 'Upgrades' section of Chapter Two.

HANDLEBAR COMPUTER

You'll quickly come to appreciate the benefits of being able to check your distance, even if it's simply as an aid to map-reading. Speed is interesting too, particularly if your ego gets the upper hand from time to time, and if you're into 'training', rather than simply riding, your computer will be witness to how you've stuck to your schedule.

BAR ENDS

Almost an essential for cross-country racers, bar ends help you to climb more efficiently by stretching your upper body and letting you use more upper body leverage and strength.

CLIPLESS PEDALS

Another popular upgrade, they add substantially to pedalling efficiency, help you to pull the back wheel up over obstacles and make full use of those expensive shoes you've just bought.

SUSPENSION

Adding a bit of weight to the bike but boosting comfort and control over tough terrain, suspension forks are probably the most popular upgrade to middle price-range bikes.

THE TOOL BOX

Many riders make do with their 'Essential Collection' tool pack. But as your enthusiasm builds, your growing mechanical knowledge will probably begin to demand a few more tools – a few too many to fit into the mobile pack. Start by buying the sort of multi-tool that includes an adjustable wrench, allen keys to fit everything on the bike, spoke key and a chain rivet extractor. Then progress to…

patch kit

HEADSET, BOTTOM BRACKET & PEDAL SPANNERS

These frequently used to come as one set, but check sizes before you buy; headsets and bottom brackets vary. Cartridge bottom brackets need very different tools to the old cup and loose bearing variety.

FREEWHEEL REMOVERS/ CASSETTE CRACKERS

Take your bike to a shop to find out what type you need. There are many sizes.

CRANK EXTRACTOR

You will usually need a bottom bracket bolt box-end wrench or allen key and an extractor tool.

WRENCHES

An all-purpose adjustable wrench, or a variety of box-end wrenches.

CLEANING FLUIDS, LUBRICANTS & GREASE

Most MTB enthusiasts will clean and lubricate their bikes after every dirty ride. It only takes about 10 minutes and it prevents all sorts of corrosion problems from setting in.

CABLE CUTTERS & CABLE END CAPS

Frayed cables are irritating and can be painful on bare flesh.

A VARIETY OF SPARE PARTS

This should include a patch kit, tubes, spokes, brake pads, brake and gear cables and a spare tire. It's a sure thing that the stores will be closed when you need them most.

multi spoke wrench

allen keys

pro crankwrench

Picking your trails

You don't have to ride up mountains to be a mountain biker — that's the beauty of it. You can be a city mountain biker, a waste ground mountain biker, a towpath mountain biker or a forest mountain biker. There are few places in the world where being a mountain biker is impossible.

Of course, every hardcore mountain biker goes on about the thrill of single-track biking or the adrenaline buzz of downhills, but for each and every single-track demon there are half a dozen riders who are happy jumping in and out of holes up in the local woods. Wherever you live, you can become a mountain biker. All you need is the right equipment and the right attitude.

Given that mountain bikers are recent trail-users compared to hikers and horses, the way you show your attitude is important. Respect all other trail-users. Smile and greet them even if they scowl at you. Don't creep up behind people; mountain bikes can be surprisingly quiet, so it's always best to ring a bell or cough as you approach from behind. Never ride too fast to be able to see your safe stopping

WHEN MEETING HORSES
Etiquette is the name of the game when meeting other trail-users. With someone on horseback, stay as still and quiet as possible, or the horse may take fright.

distance. Respect the trails — try not to skid, avoid the muddiest trails and don't ride off the edge of trails, even if the only alternative is a muddy puddle. Take all your trash home. Leave gates as you find them. Stop and do some trail maintenance from time to time, even if it's simply re-filling a hole with soil and cuttings. Always check that you have legal access to a trail.

CHOOSING A PATH
Different areas have different rights of way. Find out where you can and can't ride on your proposed route — and prevent any trouble in advance.

LOOKING AFTER YOURSELF

Wherever you go to ride, always take precautions for the worst possible scenario. Self-sufficiency is central to mountain biking. Even a late afternoon ride in the local woods could turn into a mini disaster if you fall and no one else comes by that evening. It's not likely to happen but you should at least be aware of the risk element. Some riders take a mobile phone with them, others don't go anywhere without a survival sheet in their saddle pack.

You should always be aware of what your planned route entails. Do you need a map? If you do, learn how to read it properly. Concentrate on the contours, not just the dotted red line, and remember that the weather (check the forecast) and seasonal conditions, such as mud, can slow you dramatically.

Always tell someone where you're going and roughly how long it should take. Ride within your limits. Always eat and drink plenty on longer rides. If you get hungry and thirsty, then you've probably already left it too long; food and drink takes a while to convert into warmth and energy. Always take a little more food than you think you'll need. It's a good idea to carry an extra waterproof shell in your pack on all trips. You'll need it sooner or later and it stops the tools from rattling around.

WINTER BIKING
A route that presents you with a one-and-a-half hour pleasant summer jaunt can become a four-hour endurance trial in the depths of winter.

Wilderness ways

If you're going out into uninhabited areas that are not heavily used, it's more than wise to take a few extra precautions.

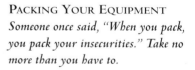

Ideally, do not ride on your own. Take far more notice of weather forecasts. Work out an exact route and tell someone what it is – don't just go out exploring, unless you're with an experienced group. Take a map. Consider your clothing more carefully. If it's cold and/or wet, take items like waterproof socks, balaclava, survival bag/blanket, a whistle and a flashing LED light. A small flashlight could be a useful extra and, if you're going anywhere that's new to you, always take a compass (and learn how to use it properly). A small first-aid kit should be carried by at least one rider. It should include bandages, painkillers and antiseptic cream. Take enough high-energy food bars for a reserve; dried fruit is a good alternative. This may sound like a lot of hassle, but it's well worth it. Once you've got these items together, you can keep them ready for subsequent trips.

A large saddle pack should hold all the stuff mentioned above. Some riders use a small backpack or a top pack on a rear rack that doubles up as a fender. If it's wet, fit your down tube with the kind of fender that will catch all the mud that can fly up as you ride along.

When you plan a wilderness ride, try to base it on recommended routes. If lots of riders have been there before, you can get a feeling for what you're letting yourself in for. Don't over-estimate your speed. On flat terrain, even the average MTB racer's speed is only about 9mph (15kph). Add hills, flat tires and tiredness and you'll soon be down to half that. For an average rider, a realistic distance to cover in a comfortable day, with a lunch stop, is around 22 miles (35km). Experienced riders may tackle up to 50 miles (80km), but rarely day after day.

PACKING YOUR EQUIPMENT
Someone once said, "When you pack, you pack your insecurities." Take no more than you have to.

RIDING OUT (left)
Getting out and about into interesting parts is what it's all about. But don't get carried away and set off into the distance without being properly prepared.

ENERGY LEVELS (right)
Remember — food and drink takes a while to convert into warmth and energy, so stop regularly.

Check before you ride

There are all sorts of things to check before you set off on a ride. If you're well organized, you'll have gone through most of the bike-related stuff after your last ride. Cleaning and maintaining a bike immediately after each ride is far less time-consuming than leaving it until just before the next excursion. Here's a list of bike checks that you should carry out on a regular basis.

1 CHECK THE TIRES

Clean the tread so that you can see any splits, thorns and so on. Check the sidewalls for bulges and damage from rubbing brakes. Make sure your tires are pumped up enough for efficient rolling. If they're too soft, they will feel squidgy and will be subject to inner tube pinch flats over rough terrain.

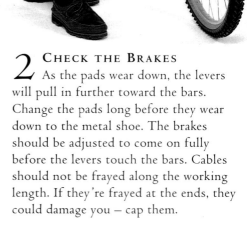

2 CHECK THE BRAKES

As the pads wear down, the levers will pull in further toward the bars. Change the pads long before they wear down to the metal shoe. The brakes should be adjusted to come on fully before the levers touch the bars. Cables should not be frayed along the working length. If they're frayed at the ends, they could damage you – cap them.

3 TIGHTNESS AND SMOOTH RUNNING

It only takes about two minutes to check every allen bolt fixing on a bike. The headset on new bikes often comes loose on the first ride as the cups settle tighter into the head tube; if you ride it loose you will ruin the bearings. The same applies to the bottom bracket and wheel bearings; check them from time to time.

4 SPIN THE WHEELS

If they're out of true, have them trued in a bike store, unless you *really* know what you're doing. Spokes often loosen on new bikes. If you find loose spokes, take the bike back to the store. Check the rims for damage. Hitting rocks can put large, flat sections in rims and it's not always possible to carry out a good repair. If your rims are old, they may be getting thin on the sides. If they start to go concave, replace them immediately.

5 CHECK THE CHAIN

Broken chains are a common cause of breakdown on the trail. Replace the chain if it doesn't sit securely on the chainring teeth. If it's been worn out for a while, the freewheel cogs will probably be worn out too. A new chain will often slip on a worn freewheel, so it's far better to replace the chain at regular intervals (perhaps around twice a year for average mountain bike riders).

6 CHECK YOUR GEAR

Finally, think about your clothing, your trail pack and whether you have enough money with you; even on short rides, always take enough cash for a phone call or a small snack. A common mistake is to forget to repair a flat inner tube that you put in your trail pack last time out. Even if you don't use your pack much, check it from time to time.

Bike transport

The real beauty of mountain biking is that, in principle, you can set off from your front door. Realistically though, not everyone wants to ride their local terrain every day of the year, especially if it's urban and bottlenecked with traffic. So, what are the alternatives?

There is no denying that driving to trails is usually the most convenient option. The ideal mountain biker's car is a hatchback or pickup. Even a moderately sized, economical-to-run hatchback can take a couple of bikes and luggage comfortably in the back. If you want to take more people and bikes, there are plenty of rack options. A roof rack has room for up to four bikes, but the wind-drag will reduce your fuel economy and it's hard work getting the bikes up there after a long ride. Trunk racks are the most popular carrying method. They can be attached to a tow bar or simply hung on the trunk lid and can carry from two to four bikes. If your rack covers the car's lights or license plate, get a tow plate that can be connected to the car's electrical system. Always lock bikes on a rack and lock the rack to the car.

ROOF-MOUNTED (*left*)
This is the cheapest way to carry bikes, but remember to watch for overhead obstacles.

TOW-HITCH MOUNTED (*below*)
The best way to carry bikes is on a purpose-made carrier, mounted on the towing hitch of your car. This solution is solid, secure and easy to load.

BY TRAIN

There aren't many places in the US where rail travel is a realistic option, but if you travel abroad, especially in Europe, trains can be the best transport method for cyclists. Planning a place-to-place trip is easy if there's a railway station at either end. Complications arise because railway systems are not always as bike-friendly as they should be. But some European countries actively encourage cyclists to use trains and offer bike rental and storage facilities at many stations. Always check with the relevant railway booking offices well before your journey. If you're willing to book a space for your bike in advance, there's usually a way, even if it means disassembling the bike and putting it in a bag.

BY PLANE

Planes usually present no problem. Airlines vary on whether they charge for bikes, and most will insist that the bike is bagged or boxed, with the air let out of its tires.

BY BUS

Buses, like trains, are not consistent. Check in advance with the bus companies and always expect to box or bag the bike. If you can get it into a reasonably sized box, it should be treated like any other piece of luggage.

RENT A BIKE

Sometimes it's easier to rent a bike when you get to a location, rather than have the hassle of transporting your own.

BIKE BOXES AND BAGS

It's usually pretty easy to persuade your local store to give you a bike-box. Many of them are thrown away anyway. For ease of handling, get the smallest box you can fit the bike into in its stripped-down state.

Specially designed bike bags are usually big enough to accommodate any bike with the wheels and pedals taken off. Most of them have side sleeves for the wheels. To keep everything as compact as possible, it's usually best to remove the quick-release skewers from the wheels, the saddle and post and the handlebar/stem assembly. These can be taped to the bike in order to stop them rattling around in transit. If you are sending the bag with an airline, assume that it will be chucked around and dropped from time to time. Pad vulnerable parts, like the crankset and the rear derailleur. Foam pipe insulaton on the frame tubes is a good extra precaution.

Basic navigation

It's amazing how easy it is to get lost on a mountain bike. Remembering obvious landmarks on local trails is one thing, but if you're out in the middle of nowhere, it's absolutely essential to be able to use a map and a compass properly.

Map-reading is pretty simple once you get the hang of it. You need to be able to read the height scales on contours so that you can find out where the hills are — the closer together the contours are, the steeper the hill. Look for obvious landmarks on the map, like rivers, buildings, monuments and trail junctions. Learn to distinguish between different types of trails;

not all rights of way will be marked in the same way, just as not all roads will be same color.

The perfect map is one that has enough detail to find your way, but not so much that you need six maps for one day trip. The bigger the number (say, 1:100,000), the greater the detail. 1:50,000 hiker maps will usually show an area about 25 miles square. That should suffice. Look after your

maps; if you're likely to be going out when it's wet, cover them with plastic or buy a laminated map in the first place. A sweaty jersey pocket can ruin a paper map in just one day.

READING MAPS
Knowing how to read a map properly will help you to make much more of your cycling — and might just get you out of a dangerous situation some day.

GETTING YOUR BEARINGS

A compass can be very useful if you're in the middle of an area with no obvious landmarks. Here's how to get your bearings:

1 Roughly line up your Magnetic North on the compass.

2 Stand with the Northern edge of the map facing North.

3 Put the compass flat on the map with the edge of its base plate lined up along your line of travel. You can find your line of travel on the map by linking your last known point with another point you are heading for.

4 Turn the compass dial until N on the dial points to North on the map.

5 Remove the compass from the map and turn yourself around until the red end of the compass needle points to N on the dial. The direction of travel arrow will now point in your direction.

6 Set off again, ideally finding a landmark along your line of travel to head towards. At each landmark you can repeat the process if you're still unsure.

RIDING RULES

We've already touched on this earlier in the chapter, but there are some things that are worth going into in a bit more detail.

• Presenting the right image makes you a mountain bike ambassador. Try to be courteous and considerate towards other trail users.

• Learn how to stop without skidding. Skids are a good excuse for other trail-users to moan about mountain bikers having no respect for nature.

• Horses have no particular reason to trust bikes. Your bright colors or fast movements can startle them. Always stop for horses and let the rider know if you are approaching from behind. Wait for a rider to wave you past; they may prefer to pull the horse off the trail to let you pass. Always leave horses as much room as possible.

• Some dogs tend to regard mountain bikers either as a plaything, or a threat. Be wary of all dogs. Most have friendly intentions but it's always best to slow or stop. Talk to the dog and the owner.

• You have as much right to be on legal trails as a hiker, but give them plenty of room, let them know you are there without surprising them, offer them the right of way and thank them if they offer it to you. Even if there is loads of room, never 'buzz' hikers. If they are not mountain bikers themselves, they may not be aware that you think you're in total control. To a non-mountain biker, a fast mountain biker looks like an out-of-control mountain biker.

• Always stay on marked trails. Going off the trails is likely to damage fragile environments, and it may be dangerous.

Problems on the trail

Every true mountain biker has had an accident. Some have several minor mishaps every time they go out. Thankfully, most accidents produce nothing more than a few scratches and bruises. But you should be aware that riding a bike is a potentially dangerous activity.

In principle, improving your skills will help to limit your mishaps, although it has to be stated that skilled riders just tend to push a bit harder, so they often have just as many spills as beginners. Learning how to fall is another way of limiting your chances of receiving a more serious injury, but you should also know exactly what to do if you do have a serious accident. Knowing how to care for yourself and how to care for others are equally important.

If you're going anywhere away from well-frequented routes, you should be fully aware of where your nearest escape routes are. Three or four rider groups are better than pairs – if an injury occurs, one or two riders can go for help while another stays with an injured rider. Mobile phones can be extremely useful.

If you are planning a serious trip into the hills, make sure a few of you are fully versed in first aid techniques.

If a rider is injured, do not move them until you are positive that their neck or back are not damaged. Leave their helmet on

DEALING WITH INJURY
Even the best riders fall. Organized races should have first aid help on hand.

but make sure the strap is not restricting their breathing. Cover them to keep them warm – that survival blanket in your saddle pack is bound to come in handy one day. If they can be moved safely, lie them on their side and support their head and neck. If you have to go for help, make sure the accident victim is as well shielded from the elements as possible and make a note of some landmarks so that you don't forget where you left them.

FIRST AID KITS

For day trips, a simple first aid kit with bandages and antiseptic cream should suffice. Insect repellent, sun lotion and antihistamine tablets are all extras to consider, depending on the season. For longer expeditions, get a full traveller's first aid kit. If you're travelling in foreign climes, read up on what you're likely to encounter there. Don't forget that one of the most important first aid essentials is energy – your emergency supply of food and water is probably more crucial than anything else.

LEARNING HOW TO FALL

Falling is something that gets easier with practice. Pick an area of soft ground and practice. After a while, you'll find out how to avoid the hard knocks.

1 As you start to fall, position yourself on the bike so that you can roll onto the ground.

2 Try to fall with several parts of your body making ground contact in a rolling motion, but with your head held slightly up.

3 Continue the roll for as long as you still have momentum. Try to lift the bike clear of your body as you lose contact with it.

On-trail repairs

It's the little things that matter in mountain biking. If you take the right tools and spare parts with you when you go riding, you should always be able to carry out fast, effective repairs.

In most cases, your trail pack will hold enough tools and spare parts to get you home again after breakdowns. But you can't take along tools and spares for every possible eventuality – sometimes you will just have to improvise. This section is about how to do just that. First, think about all those reasons why mountain bikers get stranded with a disabled bike. The common ones, listed below, are usually preventable.

• Spare tube also leaks
Always be sure you have a good spare tube or two. If the spare has been folded up in a wet and tight space for months, it may have disintergrated.

• Patch glue has dried up or run out
Once a tube of repair patch glue has been opened, the air gets in and it's not uncommon for the whole tube to dry solid or evaporate if the lid is not properly replaced.

• Spare tube has the wrong valve type
Fat Schraeder (car-type) valves will not fit through rims drilled for Presta (skinny) valves.

• Chain link tool has a bent pin
This is one of the main causes of riders being stuck in the middle of nowhere. Broken chains are more common than any other failure except flats.

Make sure your chain rivet tool is working. If not, you too will be scooting home one day.

• You've lost your tire levers
In many cases, you can get your tire off with your hands. If you can't, use a wheel/saddle quick-release lever.

USEFUL ADDITIONS TO YOUR TOOL PACK:
• Zip ties
These are bound to come in handy eventually. Use them to fasten a broken pedal together, tie freewheel

FLATS
Take your time fixing a flat. Partly inflate your repaired tube and always check the tire for the cause of the flat.

cogs to the spokes when the drive mechanism strips (creating a fixed wheel), fasten parts to the bike when a clip or bolt fails, keep a chainring or jockey wheel in position when it's lost a bolt.

• Wire, tape and toe straps
These are all useful extras that can hold things in place after a breakage (bottle cages, saddle rails and so on).

• A rag or some wet wipes
If you carry out on-trail repairs, it's good to be able to clean your hands afterward. Grass or leaves will suffice in most cases, but wet wipes are more efficient. A rag can also be used to pad out your tool kit and stop stuff from rattling.

• Little nuts and bolts
If you're going anywhere that's not within easy access of civilization, take a few spare nuts and bolts with you.

• Cables
For long tours, extra brake and gear cables may come in handy.

REMOVING THE BACK WHEEL

Before you can repair a flat it's important you know how to remove a wheel quickly and easily.

1 Loosen the brake calipers and swing the pads clear of the tire.

2 If it's a rear wheel, put the chain in the smallest freewheel cog first; then undo the quick release lever on the hub.

3 Finally, lift the bike and slide the wheel free. It may sometimes be necessary to wiggle it around a bit to clear the tire through the brake pads.

REPAIRING A FLAT

Always carry a spare tube as well as a patch kit. It is not uncommon to get more than one flat on a ride. Follow this process to replace your damaged tube:

1 Follow the procedure for removing the back wheel given on the previous page.

2 Using two tire levers, or your hands, lever one side of the tire off the rim and remove the tube.

3 Find the hole in the tube and determine what has caused it. It may be necessary to remove a thorn or something from the tire to stop it from damaging a new tube.

4 Either replace the tube with a new one or repair the damaged one. You should slightly inflate the new tube first so that it sits in place better.

6 When fitting the new tube and re-fitting the tire, take care to ensure that the tire bead is fully seated in the rim and that the inner tube is not pinched between the tire and rim.

7 Re-inflate the tube when all looks well, checking constantly that the tire is still staying seated properly on the rim.

EMERGENCIES

If you're stuck without a tube or repair patches, there are ways of making do. For example, you can cut the inner tube in half and then knot it tightly at the ends, or you can stuff the tire with leaves and grass. If the puncture is a slow one and you're close to civilization, try pumping a bit of milk into the tire; it will instantly congeal around small holes. Remember that once you've done this though – when you puncture again, the smell will be horrendous! Whichever method you choose, you'll have to ride home with extreme care.

5 If you have to patch the old tube: make sure the area around the hole is clean; sand it with the paper in the repair kit; apply the glue, smooth it with your finger, and then leave it to get tacky before applying a patch. Five minutes between glueing and patching should suffice, then another five for the patch to dry.

GET-YOU-HOME REPAIRS

With a little knowledge and imaginative innovation, you'll find that there are very few things that will totally disable your bike.

WRECKED GEARS

Sticks can grab your derailleurs and wreck them; chains can get twisted beyond the point of a simple repair; you might simply have a badly adjusted rear derailleur that pushes the chain over the big cog into the spokes. Whatever has gone wrong, a wrecked derailleur or a severely shortened usable length of chain means you need to find a new way to route the chain, as follows:

1 Split the chain with your rivet extractor.
2 Remove the rear derailleur.
3 Put the chain on the middle ring at the front and around whichever freewheel sprocket is lined up pretty straight with the middle ring.
4 Shorten and then re-join the chain, creating a single gear to get you home.

RIM STRAIGHTENING

Ordinary rim damage is usually easy to repair. The principle of rim straightening is to use a spoke nipple key to tighten the spokes on one side and loosen them on the other, thereby pulling over that part of the rim. The subtleties of this art are best left to an expert, but you can usually do enough to get you home. Heavily 'taco'd' wheels are another matter. Taco'ing, or 'crisp'ing', a wheel usually occurs during landings from jumps or when you crash and the wheel gets a heavy side impact. This is how to carry out a get-you-home repair:

1 Remove the wheel.
2 Place the wheel on the ground, with the axle resting on a solid surface and the most bent part of the rim facing upward.

BROKEN HANDLEBARS
Sticks can be very useful for emergency repairs. Here one is used to temporarily repair a broken handlebar.

3 Put one foot on the rim, where it touches the ground, and put the other foot on the bent part.
4 Push down on the bent part of the rim, bouncing and using your full body weight, until it pops back into place. It will never be perfect, but it should get you home if you loosen off the brake slightly.

BROKEN GEAR CABLES

If you snap a gear cable, front or rear, you can usually use the adjuster stop-screws on the derailleurs to set the bike in one gear for the ride home, or use a piece of wood to wedge the derailleurs in position. Bits of wood can come in handy for all sorts of things, like making a splint for a broken handlebar or frame tube.

BROKEN DERAILLEURS
Sticks can also be used to fix broken derailleurs.

CHAPTER FOUR

All-terrain techniques

'All the gear and no idea!' How many times have you heard that? Money can buy you the best MTB on the planet, but you can't buy ability. Your skills have to be learned, then developed over a period of time. Even basic fitness is a learning process for your body. You teach it how to deal with effort by taking it to various thresholds and back again. Gradually, those thresholds move. What was once a stumbling block eventually dwindles to the point of irrelevance. Keep trying to overcome thresholds and stumbling blocks and you'll discover that they only stay put if you let them.

Getting in shape

Whatever natural instincts or techniques you may have for cycling, fitness will always be an issue. There's no point developing a method for going uphill fast if you're not fit enough to push the pedals hard. And even if your genes have given you superior heart, lung and mental capacity, you still need to know how to prepare your body for the specific rigors of MTB.

In club cycling circles, getting in shape would be called 'training'. But the average mountain biker will soon realize that control and fluidity over challenging terrain are just as important as the sort of absolute speed that comes from road cyclist fitness training. Ride tough terrain with a few hills and you'll get fit in the right way. That's all

there is to it, really. Reaching a reasonable level of preliminary fitness is advisable if you want to race mountain bikes or do long-distance rides without the fun element wearing thin, but one of the greatest things about mountain bikes is that you can reach that reasonable level without going out and pounding the roads to get the miles in. Even half-hour

off-road outings will challenge your body. Chuck in a few ups and downs, and a handful of technically demanding single track, and you'll achieve the sort of body work-out that would take you

GENERAL WARM-UP
If there's a tough start to your ride, make sure you warm up thoroughly before setting off.

CAUTION

Don't stretch too far or too quickly. Stop the minute you feel any discomfort and always take it gently – never 'bounce-stretch'.

about three times as long on the road. Off-road riding is more of a full body workout than road riding. Just check out the physiques of mountain bikers compared to those of road bikers. There is no denying that, as a breed, they tend to boast altogether more 'rounded' fitness profiles.

THE PRELIMINARIES

If you're going to tackle your mountain biking as a fitness thing, you'll need to take all the usual precautions of fitness training. If you have any doubts at all about your current state of health and fitness, go and see your doctor for a check-up. Don't try vigorous exercise until you have a clean bill of health.

When you're ready to start, take it easy at the beginning. Start off by being aware of which muscles you're using on the bike. Don't forget that, if you are riding difficult terrain, you'll be using your upper body pulling muscles almost as much as your lower body pushing ones. Try to make time to stretch all those muscles gently before you venture out. Pay particular attention to stretching when the weather is cold – it's much easier to damage cold muscles. Don't 'bounce stretch'; stretch gradually without straining and relax between each stretch. Given that most fun riders will

completely ignore advice to stretch, the alternative is to take it easy at the outset. Ride some warmth into your muscles before you begin the hard stuff. Don't let your ego get the better of you on the first big uphill. Just let your friends ride ahead. You'll find that you will benefit from your slow start later in the ride.

Always take some water with you on a ride, and drink at regular intervals. If you're planning to ride for much more than an hour, it may be worth considering adding some sort of energy fuel to your water, or taking some food with you. Your usual body fuel, carbohydrate, starts to run low after about an hour-and-a-half. When that happens, you'll start to burn fat for energy. This is good

HAMSTRING STRETCH
It's always worth stretching out your muscles before a ride.

news in terms of getting fit, in pure endurance terms, but it can be bad news if you're not able to top up your immediate energy needs by eating and drinking.

The fitness level that top racers develop comes from a potent mix of training: short, fast rides for the speed benefits that come from building the power of the heart, lungs and limbs; longer, slower rides for building endurance through efficient fuel-burning. There are no short cuts to race fitness – it's a long-term, gradual process. But then, you certainly don't need race-level fitness to have fun.

Correct riding position

There is no one correct riding position, because there is no one correct body shape. We humans come in all shapes and sizes. Fortunately, most of the bike manufacturers realize this, although it has to be said that far less consideration is given to women riders than to men.

The majority of bikes are designed by men, for men. Women swivel and tilt in different places and tend to have slightly longer legs and shorter upper bodies than men of the same height, so women's bikes often need to be different. Getting a smaller frame size will sometimes suffice, but it's not always the best solution. As you come to understand how different ride positions suit you, or not, as the case may be, you'll find that the manufacturers' assumptions may not suit your style. You'll learn as you go along, and what is right for you now may not be right when you start to gain fitness or tackle more radical terrain.

MTB SHAPES

In theory, there is very little difference between the shape of a normal beginner's MTB and the fanatic's MTB. Components will inevitably vary, but the only major thing you'll notice in ride position terms is that the experienced mountain bikers may develop a more stretched ride posture on the bike. Up-market MTB top tubes tend to be longer, allowing riders to develop a more efficient full-body stretch across the bike. This helps the rider to pull on the bars more effectively when climbing, especially when standing. If you climb while standing on a bike with a short top tube and a short high-rise stem, then you can't put as much leverage power through your upper body, so your legs become less efficient at driving the bike.

It could be argued that the main reason beginner MTBs offer short ride postures and higher front ends, is that most beginners initially feel more at ease with a ride position that comes closer to the walking stance. It could also be argued that beginners have not yet developed their upper body cycling muscles to a level where a racer stretch feels comfortable. Aspects of both those arguments are undoubtedly used by manufacturers who want to separate their beginner ranges from more advanced models. But for those of you who want to make fast progress off-road, you will soon feel the need for the more advanced posture that comes with mid- and top-of-the-range bikes.

THE FRAME SPECIFICS

As we have already explained in Chapter 2, bike sizing is a confusing issue. There are four or five different ways of measuring a frame in order to attach a size listing to it, and there's often no way of knowing which method a bike manufacturer has chosen.

Some measure the seat tube from the center of the bottom bracket to the center of the top tube where it joins the seat tube. Some measure to the center of an imaginary horizontal top tube where it would join the seat tube. Some measure to the top of the seat tube. Some measure to the top of the top tube where it joins the seat tube. Confused? Most of us are, and it doesn't get any easier. Top tube lengths are measured in several different ways too, as are frame angles when suspension is included in the overall equation.

The measurements that actually matter on a mountain bike are the cockpit length and the standover height. You'll just have to assume that the manufacturer has got the frame angles right. Cockpit length is the distance between the seatpost center and the handlebar center, and it determines how far your body has to stretch from the saddle to the handlebars. Getting the right cockpit length relates principally to your upper body and arm length; moving the saddle up, down, back and forth changes cockpit length, as does changing your stem. Standover height determines crotch clearance when you're straddling the top tube. There are times when you'll be straddling the top tube when you don't want to be, so it's essential to have at least 2-3 inches' crotch clearance when you stand over the middle point of the top tube.

LITTLE THINGS THAT MATTER

Choosing a bike with the right cockpit length and standover height is a function of trial and error. Although there are formulas to apply, few of them are accurate

in practice. The most common MTB bike size formula is 'inside leg minus 13in (33cm)', but just stop and think about this one. This formula would mean that someone with an 32in (81cm) inside leg would ride a 19in frame. That's probably about right, but where has the manufacturer measured the 19in to? And if the rider is female, the top tube on a 19in frame could be too long.

Trial and error is the only real solution. Ride a friend's bike; try out demo models in shops. Choose a bike that makes you feel nicely balanced, but not one where you have to reach with your whole body to apply the brakes or move to the bar ends. The saddle should feel about right in its center post position. Here are some more points to consider about bike set-up:

SADDLE
Your saddle should be almost perfectly level. The right height is when your leg is slightly bent at the bottom of every pedal stroke. A slightly lower saddle position is better for difficult trails; pure down-hillers drop their saddles down by up to 3 in (8 cm).

STEM
As a rule, don't buy a bike that needs a much longer stem than the 'standard' one fitted — long stems can upset steering characteristics.

BRAKE/SHIFT LEVERS
Levers should be placed for comfy access. If you have to move your hand position or reach for them, they're probably badly positioned.

SEATPOST
If your frame is the right size, you should have about 6-9 in (15-23 cm) of seat post showing above the seat tube with enough supportive length remaining inside the main frame triangle.

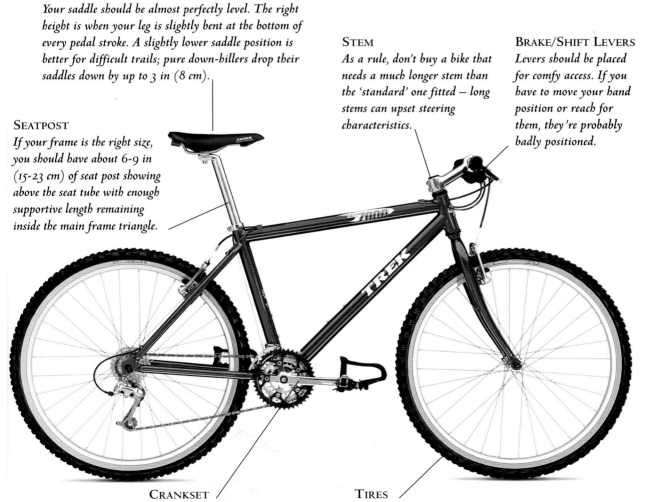

CRANKSET
Crank lengths vary. The most common are 170 or 175 mm. As a rule, riders with an inside leg length under 30 in (76 cm) should choose 170 mm cranks.

TIRES
How much air is in your tires will substantially affect the way the bike handles. Too little air makes the bike slow, squirmy and subject to flats. Too much makes it skittish and challenged in traction. Check the tire walls.

Biking techniques

As you start to incorporate gradual learning stages into the flow of the trail, you'll be surprised at how quickly all those little jerky movements of the practice process can become a smooth, almost instinctive, part of your riding. Practice is the key. You'll soon be a better rider.

W e're going to start with what seems like a very simplistic approach – learning how to balance, brake, climb, descend, corner and change gear. This may seem condescending to some, but a large number of beginners need some help getting to grips with these basics. We'll leave the 'how to pedal' bit to your imagination.

TRACKSTANDING
Learning how to come to a standstill and balance the bike is one of the most crucial prerequisites of advanced technique training.

CONTROL
Using your body to shift the bike's center of balance from side to side will help you line up for obstacles and difficult corners. These are essential techniques for slow speed maneuvers.

BALANCE

A better description of balance would be 'correct weight distribution'. As speeds increase, balance becomes easier, but you'll spend much of your MTB time at slow speeds, trying to overcome trail difficulties. The first trick is to find out what you can and can't do.

Spend time playing on your bike at slow speeds. Ride even slower than you need to ride, perhaps coming to a standstill at times, just for the practice. Try to develop your abilities at turning slow, tight circles, riding over rocks, performing sudden small spurts forward and controlling precise movement of the bike with the brakes. Get a feel for how the front and rear brakes affect the bike in different ways. Then try all

of this at different speeds, in different gears and over different terrain types – but at all times concentrating on perfect balance.

Gradually increase your speed. When you can do things slowly, you will find that they often become easier at speed. Try different climbing techniques, sitting and standing or pushing different gears. Try moving your body around on the bike, leaning more into corners rather than relying on steering. Develop a sense for how bike control changes when you sit further forward or further back on the saddle. Try everything at least once. It's the best way to learn about what the bike can do. You'll be surprised at times, and you'll find out all kinds of things really quickly. Even the

most experienced riders play around like this. Minor changes on a bike, like changing stem length or saddle height, can really alter the way the bike feels to you.

BRAKING

First, notice that the left hand lever operates the front brake and the right hand lever the rear. This is standard on all bicycles, as it allows you to operate the rear brake while signalling to traffic with your left hand. Your front brake is your most powerful braking force. You use the rear brake for additional and more precise control over speed and balance. Braking is the most important rider/bike interaction to learn. Get used to the reactions of the bike when you brake on different surfaces. Get to

PRACTICING CONTROL
Mini slalom. Set up a few rocks on a downhill slope and ride between them. This is ideal practice for slow-speed cornering and precise balance.

know when the wheels will lock. There are times when you will want to lock the rear wheel, but it would be a very rare thing if you actually chose to lock the front wheel, as this almost always causes you to fall. Brake with the front and rear brakes individually, just to get a feel for it, and then try combination braking, using varying force. Try 'feathering' the brakes (a gentle on-and-off action). Skid-free stops will almost always be the best stops. Apart from anything else, you won't leave your mark.

On steep, loose or slippery descents, you may be able to exert some power through the front brake, but the rear brake becomes more crucial in control terms. When you're braking hard on the front, steering control will always be slightly hindered. Set up a mini slalom course to learn the basics of downhill braking whilst steering. There are times when releasing the brakes and gaining speed on a corner will be the only way to get around

safely without loosing traction. Heavy braking is always better done on the straights. Reduce your speed to a controllable rate before corners. If you have to brake on corners, only do it gently. The art of good braking is anticipation. Keep it smooth and under control and never leave it until the last second.

CLIMBING
Correct climbing technique is almost as important as fitness. Steering a slow and bumpy uphill course is one of the hardest MTB skills, and going hard and fast is the most physically demanding aspect of off-roading. For slow, technical climbs, try to pick a line

that avoids obstacles, or one that chooses minor obstacles in order to avoid the major ones. To change your line, simply shift your weight. Use only slight movement of the handlebars; big front end movements will tip you off-balance.

Try to stay sitting so that your body weight is well over the back wheel, for better traction. If you can stand without losing traction, the steering may become easier, but attempt to hover just above the saddle rather than standing forward. Good technical climbing is just a question of good weight distribution and correct gear choice. Correct gear choice will come with practice, but you should always be in a gear that avoids 'dead' spots as you make each crank rotation. Faster rotations will almost always be better than hauling the cranks around slowly, but sudden stabs of power can cause wheel spin and a consequent loss of balance and momentum.

For short, sharp steep sections, or the sort of technical sections that appear to offer no obvious line through, try to increase your speed as you approach. A speed boost will often

get you over the tough parts by using momentum rather than skills. If a climb has a few tough sections interspersed with easier parts, soft-pedal on the easier sections so that you can power-pedal through the difficult ones.

On longer climbs, try to stay seated. Only stand, even on steeper parts, when you want to keep a pedalling cadence or if you need a change of

rhythm. In theory, you can conserve more energy by staying seated and choosing a speed that you feel comfortable with. A great way of boosting your recovery rate while getting fitter is to accelerate over the top of climbs rather than slowing or stopping, the more natural response.

CLIMBING
The skill of climbing on loose terrain is to find a perfect compromise between balance and power. You often need to stand, but you also need to keep your weight well over the saddle to stop the rear wheel spinning out.

DESCENDING

Downhilling is an integral part of cross-country riding and a discipline in itself. The art of good descents utilizes all your other skills as well as a high degree of fitness and nerve. Despite the 'brain-out' tag that they're often tainted with, the best downhillers need to be totally aware of how their bodies, their bikes and their terrain are interacting. For a beginner, the skill of becoming a good descender is to stay relaxed. A relaxed body will absorb the bumps better and will respond much more naturally to changes of terrain and direction.

While your body relaxes, your mind can work overtime. You should always look a few seconds ahead of your line in order to anticipate the way the bike will act over the next stretch of terrain. Always be ready to lift your weight off the bike over the rocky stuff. Look for the best exits from difficult sections before you enter them. As you master the more advanced skills, like front wheel lifts and hopping, you'll find that the more difficult line choices start to open up for you on descents. The faster you're travelling, the more difficult steering becomes. You will learn how to lean more into corners, so you'll start to find the traction limits of your tires. Fast descents is an educational experience!

Slow technical descents are a different matter altogether. They involve perfect balance control, very careful braking, a controlled rear wheel skid or two and a body position that slides further back as the descent steepens, often going right over the back of the saddle for extreme drops. Obstacle avoidance is advisable but if you must ride over rocks, roots and holes, let your speed increase slightly as you do so; with your body well back, the front of the bike should be light enough to bump over minor obstacles.

BRAKING ON DESCENTS (*left*)
Finding the correct braking balance on loose descents is tricky. Use the rear brake to help you maneuver and use the front brake more heavily when you're travelling straight and the surface is firm enough to reduce speed.

DESCENDING STEEP SLOPES (*right*)
Cover both brakes, keep your body weight well over the back of the bike and keep your gaze on what's ahead.

CORNERING

Cornering at slow speeds is just an extension of basic balance technique. You soon get a feel for how far you should lean and how far you should turn the steering. Cornering at high speed is an art in itself. Always let your outside pedal drop right down as you lean into a corner. Try to do all your braking before the corner, then choose the firmest looking line through the turn. Ideally, cut across the apex of the corner — go from the outside to the inside, then back out again as you emerge. Look for berms and camber changes on the corner. You can often use a positive camber to guide your wheels around the bend as you lean. There are times when the berm that forms on the outside edge of a well-used bend provides a safer line than the apex.

SLOW CORNERING
(above)
Cover both brakes but never apply the front brake too heavily. A limited skid with the back brake will sometimes help you get round the corner. Keep your body weight well back.

USING CONTOURS
(BERMS) *(left)*
The banks of earth that form around the sides of corners can often be used to good effect, helping to steer you round a corner without having to steer or lean too heavily.

CHANGING GEAR

Always try to change gear shortly before you reach the section of trail where the gear is crucial. Although modern gears are super-efficient at shifting under load, you're still better off pre-selecting gears for steep climbs rather than pushing too big a gear into the first slopes. If you're approaching a bend or a difficult section where you're likely to slow down drastically, select a gear that will be right for pulling away again.

For non-pedalling descents, always put your chain in the big ring to prevent excessive chain slack over the bumps, but remember to change gear in plenty of time for the inevitable surge back up again at the bottom. Try not to use extreme gears, like big ring, big cog or small ring, small cog; they will put everything under unnecessary strain.

Now we can progress to a few simple techniques that will add skill, fun and challenge to all your rides.

WHEN TO CHANGE GEAR
Don't wait until you're on top of an obstacle or on a steep slope before you change gear. Shift to a larger cog at the back just before you enter a difficult section, even if you are braking at the same time. With practice, this comes naturally.

Log pulls and jumps

Logs, rocks, roots, troughs, broken glass, dog food, basking animals. They're all the sort of trail obstacles that you'd be better off flying over.

The best way to learn about how to avoid such trail detritus is to treat it all as a curb. Can you hop over a curb without injuring yourself and the bike? If not, read on. Bear in mind that if you try too hard to do this kind of stuff you'll stiffen up, pull muscles, fall off and generally make a complete fool of yourself trying to do what doesn't come naturally. You should start by

watching those who are better than you. After that, practice with a mobile log, one that moves if you get it wrong.

First, come to terms with the fact that lifting your body weight away from the bike while pulling up on the bars is a totally rational damage limitation reaction to seeing a curb, a log or a rock sitting directly in your path. You've probably been doing invisible wheelies and bunny hops for ages without even realizing it. Even if you haven't actually left the ground yet, your upward weight shift will have been enough to reduce your body load on the bike when

bumping over obstacles.

Now the practical stuff starts. Think about curbs. Do you ride straight into them? If you do, you probably have no idea how to perform the log pull. The log pull, and the follow-through when you lift your body weight off the back wheel, are important moves for future progression. They'll come naturally to anyone who has mastered the body weight shifts that are essential to basic trail riding technique.

As you approach the log, bend your arms slightly and pull up on the bars to lift the front wheel up and over the obstacle. Then immediately lift your weight off the saddle to reduce weight on the back wheel at that crucial moment, just before the back wheel touches the log. A slight pull up and back on the pedals will help to lighten the back of the bike.

PROGRESSING TO JUMPS

As you progress with smoothing out the lifts and drops, you can start moving onto jumps. You'll need absolute confidence to clean-jump a log because you'll need approach speed as well as almost simultaneous front and rear wheel lift. In practice, always use an obstacle that will move or absorb the impact if you get

the jump wrong. The ideal bunny hop practice rig is two stones or bricks with a stick balanced across the top. To start with 3 inches (8 cm) will probably be high enough. Once you've really got to grips properly with this, then your step-by-step learning program is over — if you can do a mini wheely and the small bunny hop, the rest will follow naturally.

SIMPLE LOG PULL

1 Pull up on the bars to lift the front wheel up and over the obstacle.

2 Lift your weight off the saddle to reduce weight on the back wheel at the crucial moment, just before the back wheel touches the log.

3 A slight pull up and back on the pedals will help to lighten the back of the bike.

4 Let the rear wheel follow through and lift the back slightly by 'clawing' your feet on the pedals.

THE ADVANCED LOG PULL

The advanced log pull is only a short step away from a full wheely or a bunny hop. The wheely and the bunny hop are simply exaggerated versions of what you have to do to get safely over small obstacles. The bigger the obstacle, the more lift you need. A wheely demands a timely pull up on the bars with a corresponding push on the pedals for extra height. A bunny hop just combines what you are doing to get the front and back wheels over an obstacle independently.

For independent front and back wheel lifts, try practicing on a curb or a small drop-off. Try riding both up and down (riding down bumps can be made smoother using almost identical weight shift techniques) with and without the pedal-push effect. Think about what's happening when that push on the pedals gets you extra front end height. There are times when you'll need that height. Unless you can rapidly shift your weight up and forward after a mini wheely, the back wheel will just slam into the obstacle. Keep experimenting with weight shifts.

Try doing the front end bar pull and the back end saddle lift and pedal pull in quick succession. If you keep trying, you will soon find a body position that allows you to effect both moves almost simultaneously, effectively 'un-weighting' the front and back wheels at the same time. You may not leave the ground to start with, but you'll be pulling enough weight off the wheels to make the bike skip over the obstacle, rather than slamming into it. SPD-type pedals are a major boon to leaving the ground because they allow you to pull the bike straight up under your body, using your shoes as hooks.

CURB HOPPING
A slight twist on the advanced log pull will allow you to pull stunts like this, surprisingly useful at times. You don't actually need this much height though.

ADVANCED LOG PULL

1 As you approach the log, think about getting your body into a position that will allow you to pull the back wheel a bit higher than the simple log pull.

2 You don't need this much height, but it's good for practice. The idea is to get a feel for lifting the front and back wheels independently.

3 Practice dropping the front wheel then immediately lifting the back, using the same technique as in the simple log pull.

4 As you learn to lift the back more effectively, you'll be able to clear the log completely. Your next move is to convert the two lifts into one flowing movement.

Advanced techniques

A lot of advanced technique will come naturally through learning basic technique. As we've already explained, little front wheel lifts can soon become wheelies and little back wheel lifts can very soon combine with front wheel lifts to become bunny hops and jumps. But what about when you come across terrain that simply looks like a series of insurmountable obstacles? And what about when you want to build more speed into your basic techniques?

DROP-OFFS

Some drop-offs can simply be ridden, letting the front drop over as you shift your body weight back slightly on the bike. But as drop-offs get bigger, you may have to think about more extreme solutions. If a drop-off has an easy run-out, you can usually get away with just dropping in with your weight over the back of the saddle. Even a big drop-off can be tackled like this if the transition is to an easier slope and the crankset doesn't ground on the edge of the drop-off.

If the chainrings are likely to make contact with the ground on a drop-off, or if the transition does not allow an easy run-out, you'll have to wheely off the drop-off. As you approach the edge of the drop, lift your front wheel and push hard on the pedals; ideally your front wheel should lift about 6 in (15 cm) higher than the rear. Keep pedalling until your rear wheel clears the edge of the drop-off, then get your body ready to absorb the impact of the landing. This means getting ready to bend your legs from their full extension to absorb the shock, then dropping the front of the bike down, just like finishing a wheelie. When you want to control your speed during this maneuver, you'll have to keep the rear brake covered. Don't lean back too much; you'll flip the bike over backward.

DROP-OFF

However big or small a drop-off is, the skill is to put your weight right over the back wheel, stretch your arms and keep the front of the bike light enough to effect a smooth transition back onto flat terrain.

Wheely Drop-off

This one's either for showing off, or when there is no smooth transition to flat ground. The idea is to land the rear wheel slightly before the front, absorbing the impact with your legs and, to a lesser extent, your arms.

THE SPEED JUMP

This is a smart move when you're riding the sort of terrain that makes you lift off when you don't want to. It's a great way of maintaining speed over 'jumpy' terrain; you'll always go faster if you can stay on the ground and keep pedalling. All you have to do is stand up as a potential launch hump approaches. Just before you hit the hump, lift your front wheel slightly, only enough to stop it rising up the slope of the bump. The intention is to place your front wheel just over the bump as your back wheel starts to rise. At that point, the rear wheel will rise under you. Try to keep your body level with the ground, letting the saddle rise up toward your chest as it crests the hump. With practice, you can keep pedalling hard all the way through this maneuver.

SPEED JUMPS

The idea of a speed jump is to lift your front wheel before a bump does it for you. Lift yourself off the saddle to do this then, as the front wheel drops again on the other side of the bump, let the rear wheel rise to meet your level body. With practice you can keep pedalling hard all the way through this move.

THE PRE-JUMP

When the ground drops away, you don't always want to launch yourself into the air. The safest, and fastest, way to take a potential launch pad at speed is to pre-jump it. All you have to do is to perform a little bunny hop before the lip of a drop, so that you're already coming down as you crest it. The idea is to stay close to the ground, rather than letting the lip launch you into barely controlled orbit. With practice, you can choose whether to drop the bike straight onto the down slope, or to continue that little bit of air time. Your body will be hovering, crouched over the bike, so you can lift or drop the bike slightly for exact control.

THE PRE-JUMP
If you don't want to let the lip of a hump launch you into the air, jump the bike slightly before the lip, landing on the down slope. This ensures that you lose no time or control when you're in the air.

HIGH-SPEED CORNERING

There are all sorts of variables to be considered when cornering at high speed. How firm and predictable is the terrain surface? How hard or soft should your tires be? How much can you lean without laying the bike down? Do you need to put one leg out for stabilizing? You'll never know all this stuff until you can read the terrain, and that takes time and plenty of trial and error.

Assuming that you don't really know at exactly what point the tires are going to break away from the surface as you lean into a corner, putting one foot out is always a safer technique. It helps your center of gravity and creates an immediate tripod if your tires break away and you don't want to hit the ground with your whole body. High tire pressures will not help in cornering. If the tire can distort more it will grip better.

As usual, do your braking before the corner, although bear in mind that there are times when a rear wheel skid half way around the corner can tighten your turn if you're heading for the edge. As you start to lean into the corner, make sure your inside pedal is at the 12 o' clock position; this helps to maintain traction if you very consciously push the outside pedal down toward the ground and in toward the bike. Lean your bike more than your body; this becomes more extreme as the speed increases. Leaning is better than steering because, if you steer too much, you will lose control and flip over the front. Always try to cut across the whole trail to lessen the severity of the corner.

TAKING A CORNER
Always assess your line through a corner as you approach it. Keep your outside pedal at the six o'clock position, keep your body steady and keep the brakes covered but, ideally, not applied. All your braking should be done coming into the corner. If you need to tighten up the turn, skidding the rear wheel slightly or leaning more will help.

Around town

The mountain bike is the perfect town bike. It could even be argued that the commercial success of the mountain bike lies in its ability to tackle urban landscapes far more effectively than its skinny-tire counterparts. You'll find yourself using all your off-road skills when you ride around town, and a few more besides.

The best town cyclists are motorists. The best town motorists are cyclists. If you've done both, you will have a greater understanding of what both pilots are likely to do. Motorists and cyclists have blind spots. There are often too many things to look at to be able to take in a 360-degree perspective at all times. Bear this in mind and you'll always be ready for the unexpected. With a little imagination, riding in traffic can be a genuine challenge, and you can soon become an expert.

Try to read the faces and actions of other road-users and pedestrians. If you become a part of the moving mass, you'll be surprised at how well you can use it to your advantage. When traffic accelerates, you should try to accelerate with it (within reason). Always make your intentions clear to motorists. Ride defensively. Hold your line unless you genuinely feel in danger. Exaggerate signals and try to catch the eyes of motorists as you maneuver. Don't tempt drivers into trying to squeeze past; stay out of the gutter. Don't always believe a car's indicators. Be ready for a driver to cut across your line if you're riding close to corners.

SHARING THE ROAD
Riding in traffic can be a challenge, but you can soon become an expert.

RIDE DEFENSIVELY
Try to catch the eyes of motorists as you maneuver. If you become part of the moving mass, you'll be surprised at how well you can use it to your advantage.

DRESS TO BE SEEN
Wear bright clothing and cover yourself with reflective stuff at night.

URBAN TECHNIQUES

- Learn how to shout. A good bellow is usually far more effective than a bell or a stifled curse.
- Always assume that motorists will do something unexpected. Prepare your reactions. Watch out for side streets in particular.
- Look out for parked cars with someone in them. You should expect a door to open at any time, so give them a wide berth.
- If there's no room for someone to overtake, fake a wobble to make the driver think twice if they're thinking of squeezing past.
- Practice emergency stops without skidding. If you feel competent at bunny hops, learn to do sideways ones that will get you up onto a curb if you're being squeezed.
- Wear bright clothing and cover yourself with reflective stuff at night.
- Never ride alongside a vehicle on the inside if there's even a remote chance that the driver may pull in toward the curb. Remember that articulated vehicles cut across corners dramatically.
- Smile at motorists if they're kind to you. It may even make the unkind ones realize that we're not urban terrorists.

CHAPTER FIVE

Maintaining your bike

Mountain bikes need servicing to keep them in good condition. Riding through mud and water strips the lubricant out of components, which also get covered with grime all too easily, affecting performance. To keep your bike in top condition, it's important to set aside a little time to check things over. It's far better to do this after a ride, rather than immediately before the next. If you've only got a couple of hours to ride, then you don't want to be spending half that time fiddling with wrenches and oil.

Cleaning your bike

There are some riders who insist on cleaning their bike to showroom conditions after every ride. This isn't really necessary, but you do need to know how to clean your bike in a sensible and effective way, in order to keep it running smoothly.

The motorist's favorite way of cleaning a car, the jet-wash, is used by some riders to simply blast all the dirt off their frames just by inserting the right tokens, pointing the water-gun and firing. And true enough, their frames will be clean, but chances are that the bearings in their bikes will have all the grease blasted out of them, and water blasted into them.

The best, if less dramatic, way to clean a bike is to use a bucket and brush, and the gentler pressure of a garden hose to rinse away the dirt. This allows you to keep a far better control on what water is going where, and so extend the life of your bike, by keeping lubricants, rather than water, in your bike's bearings.

1 With the hose, wet the bike all over, then, with a plastic bristled brush, like the sort of thing you'd clean a car with, start to scrub the frame tubes, handlebars and stem, tires... anywhere that's particularly grubby.

2 Attack the drive-train of the bike, scrubbing the chainrings, cogs, chain and derailleurs, using a stiffer bristled brush if you can. Specially formulated cleaners are good for these greasier areas, products such as Gunk or bicycle equivalents are well worth considering.

3 Clean the mud away from the top surface of the brake pads, as mud collecting here can wear the tire sidewalls down and cause problems.

4 Rinse the bike off with the hose, and leave it to dry.

5 After half an hour or so, use a water-repelling lubricant (such as WD40) to ensure that there is no water in the chain. WD40 isn't suitable for extended use as a chain oil, but it's good to use as a repellent, before other chain oil is added over the top.

6 The obsessives can then clean the frame tubes with a cotton rag, even polishing the frame if they're really keen. But it's not essential. Keeping the drive-train clean can prolong the life of these expensive components.

Maintaining the chain

If your chain is rusty, then it's fairly obvious that something's wrong, but you can't just oil a chain and expect it to last forever.

Chains are part of the drive-train system, running on the chainrings and the rear cogs. As the chain wears, more freeplay develops in each link. This play means that instead of the load from the chain being spread over the whole of the cog or chainring, it's concentrated on fewer teeth. This wears the cogs faster, eating away at the teeth and causing the chain to slip under load. Leave things to get really bad and a new chain won't even mate properly with the cogs.

To check for chain wear, measure the distance between twelve links. Each link should be 1in long, but the wear of the chain over twelve links will mean that a worn chain measures about $12\frac{1}{8}$in. To prolong the life of your whole drive train, chains should be changed when they have stretched to more than $12\frac{1}{16}$in.

Chains should also be kept well lubricated to limit wear. Bicycle oils are formulated to have the correct properties of penetration, film strength, dirt repellence and wash-off-ability. A good bike oil can't be too wet, or it'll attract dirt. It shouldn't wash off easily in streams, and it should keep working under a high load.

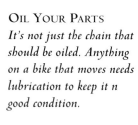

OIL YOUR PARTS
It's not just the chain that should be oiled. Anything on a bike that moves needs lubrication to keep it n good condition.

CLEAN AND DRY
Once you have lubricated the chain, wait about ten minutes before wiping away the excess oil. This will prevent the chain from attracting dirt.

HOW TO REMOVE AND INSTALL A CHAIN

To remove and install a chain, you'll need a chain tool. Shimano chains also require the use of special rivetted joining pins, which ensure the integrity of the chain if you have to break the chain at a link and then rejoin it. It's a more complicated system (other chains don't require these pins), but the advantage is that Shimano chains shift extremely well.

1 Select the link that you want to break, on the chain run between the bottom of the rear derailleur and the chainrings. Position the chain tool, and wind it inwards, pressing the link all the way through the chain.

2 Size the chain. Wrap the chain around the big chainring, and the biggest cog at the rear, then add two links for perfect length. Add two more links on a suspension bike. Remove links on the side of the chain without the rivet.

3 Install the chain. Thread the chain through the front and rear derailleurs, and let it hang over the bottom bracket. Press the pin into place with the chain tool.

4 Loosen stiff links. Either use the chain tool plate or flex the chain with your fingers.

Attending to brakes

The brakes on your bike won't work forever. If you notice more lever travel than before, or you're just getting a feeling of not stopping, then it's time to take a look at your braking system. The two parts that are going to go awry are the cables and the pads.

ADJUSTING BRAKE CABLES

The most frequent adjustment you're going to have to make is to take up the slack in the brake cables. As the pads wear, more cable is needed to be pulled through to get the pads to the rim. This can be adjusted by winding out the adjuster at the handlebar, but a better way is to actually pull the slack through at the brake, leaving the adjusters for fine tuning.

1 If you can almost pull the lever back to the handlebar, then it's too much.

2 On V brakes, loosen the cable clamp bolt.

CANTILEVERS

On cantilever brakes, loosen the cable from the straddle hanger. Pull the cable through until the pads are almost touching, then re-center the straddle hanger.

3 Pull the cable through so that the pads are almost touching the rim, then re-tighten.

4 Finally, center the brakes using an allen key or screwdriver.

REPLACING BRAKE PADS

Brake pads are the other problem. As they rub against the rim to slow the bike down, they're worn away. To start with, this will just result in a cable-slackening problem, but after a while there'll be no brake pad left. There are three types of brake pad available, each specific to their own brake. If possible, take your bike along to the shop to make sure that you get the right sort of pad for your brakes. These are the three most common types.

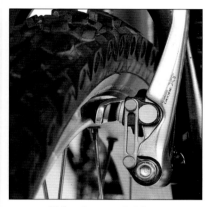

V brake cartridge

V BRAKE CARTRIDGE PADS

Release the cable from the brake by lifting the tube out of the guide. Use a pair of pliers to pull the pin out of the brake pad holder. Pull the brake pad out of the holder and replace, positioning the pad so that it hits the rim squarely and doesn't touch the tire.

BOLT-IN V BRAKE PADS

Once you have released the cable from the brake, loosen the allen nut at the back of the brake arm. Withdraw the brake pad, noting the positioning of spacers. V brakes use two different sizes of spacer, one on the inside, one on the outside. Note which is wider, and where it is. Replace the pad with the spacers in the right place. Position the pad so that it hits the rim squarely and doesn't touch the tire.

Bolt-in V brake pad

CANTILEVER PADS

Release the straddle cable and loosen the 10mm nut on the back of the brake. Remove the pad, and install a new pad half way along its shaft. Swing the cantilever up to the rim, and get the pad to hit the rim squarely. Then start to tighten the 10mm nut while holding the pad in position. Make sure everything is tight, and nothing touches the tire. To limit squeaking, the front of the brake pad should hit the rim just before the back.

Cantilever pad

BRAKE LEVERS

If your brake levers are set in the wrong position, you'll have to bend your wrists uncomfortably to reach the brake levers.

1 Loosen the allen bolt that clamps the brake lever in place.

2 Position the brake levers between 30 and 45 degrees downward, so that they're straight with your arms when you're riding.

3 If you've got large hands, slide the brake levers inwards up to a couple of centimeters from the grips. This makes shifting and braking far more comfortable.

4 When you've finished tuning the positioning, tighten the allen bolt securely.

Loose headsets

Loose headsets make themselves known when the front of the bike rattles while going over bumpy ground or when braking. When the bike is stationary and the front brake is applied, the bike will rock on the headset bearings, which will be felt through the handlebars. This rocking is due to the bearings not being loaded properly, and will result in the headset wearing out prematurely as it slams backward and forward. Adjusting the headset to the correct position will mean that the bearings are properly loaded.

There are two standards of headset on a mountain bike, which are quite different. This means that the fork, stem and headset for each system will only work within that system, and you can't use parts for one headset with another. The most common is called 'Aheadset' and does have advantages – it's not a thing that you'd set out to replace just to have a better system. Aheadset systems have no threads on the steerer tube, and rely on the stem clamping in place to keep everything snug and lined up correctly. They save a bit of weight over a conventional setup, and are also much less tool-intensive to adjust; they require just one 5mm allen key, rather than two large wrenches for the older threaded headset system. Changing to Aheadset from the threaded system requires switching the stem, fork and headset – something that's expensive to do on its own, but worth considering if you're changing the setup at the front of your bike.

The other sort of headset is variously known as a 'threaded' or 'quill-stem' headset. The bearing cups are pressed into the frame, just as for an Aheadset, but the adjustable cup of the headset is mounted on a thread on the outside of the fork steerer tube. A large locknut is used to clamp the headset up tight after adjustment. The stem clamps in place inside the steerer tube with an expanding wedge system.

5mm allen bolt in top of stem

clamp-on stem

AHEADSET SPOTTING TIPS
It is easy to spot Aheadsets. Instant giveaways include the clamp-on stem and allen bolt in the top of the stem.

AHEADSET PROBLEMS

Problems can occur if the nut in the steerer tube that the bolt pulls against has loosened. In this case, tightening the bolt will mean that, instead of applying pressure to the stem, all you're doing is simply pulling the nut upwards. This requires a new nut in the steerer tube.

The other common problem could be that the steerer tube is cut too long, and that the stem cannot slide down any further, as the steerer is resting on the cap that the bolt sits in. This can be cured by adding a spacer under the stem.

ADJUSTING AHEADSETS

1 Loosen the clamp bolt on the stem. Shift the stem from side to side a little to make sure that it's not corroded and become stuck to the steerer tube.

2 Tighten the bolt in the top of the steerer tube, to pull the stem downward, taking the slack out of the bearings. Check this by rocking the bike, and checking for bearing play.

3 To check you have not overtightened the bearings, simply pick the bike up to see if the front turns freely. Overtightening causes the bearings to be crushed and damaged.

ADJUSTING THREADED HEADSETS

1 Place your two wrenches on the headset. One on the threaded locknut at the top, and one on the adjustable cup at the bottom.

2 Undo the locknut, by holding the moveable cup spanner still and turning the other counter clockwise.

3 Tighten the adjustable cup clockwise, rocking the bike, feeling when the play just disappears.

4 Holding the adjustable cup still, and holding the front wheel between your legs to stabilize it, tighten down the locknut. Check again for bearing play, or overtightness, and repeat until correct.

checking for bearing play

Tires and wheels

Mountain bike wheels might look just like huge, tough chunks of rubber that can cope with anything, but you'll find that taking a bit of time setting up the tires on your bike can reap really valuable benefits.

If the tires aren't inflated properly, and are too soft, then you'll be at risk of suffering pinch flats when hitting rocks or sharp edges on the trail. Also, traction will suffer if you either have your tires too hard or too soft.

Check to see that the brake pads aren't rubbing on the sidewalls, and that there aren't any splits or tears in the casing. Though the tire might be holding together with a slit in it,

CHECKING TIRE PRESSURE
Simply squeeze with your thumb to check whether your tire pressure is correct.

it could rupture at the least opportune moment, and cause another flat scenario that's best avoided.

Checking tire pressure is a skill learnt with experience. It's a matter of squeezing the tire with your thumb, and feeling how hard it is. Some riders use pumps with pressure gauges to determine the pressure in their tires, but these are frequently inaccurate, and always open to misreading. A squeeze with your thumb is a foolproof method of checking pressure and works well. If you're determined to use a pressure gauge, inflate the tire to between 40 and 55psi, with higher pressures being used for smaller tires, heavier riders and faster speeds.

If you want to change your tires, there's no problem. Practically any mountain bike tire will fit on any mountain bike rim; there's nothing to worry about between brands of bike, or types of tire. The reason there are so many different types of tire is that there are different types of terrain to ride on, and each tire company makes a model of tire that's specific for certain types of terrain. Ask the local stores what's good in your area.

WHEELS

Mountain bike wheels, when protected by (properly inflated)

tires are far tougher than those on other bikes. Providing they're properly built, and those tires have enough air in them, they'll last for at least a year of hard riding.

However, hard landings and big bumps can make them bend. Wheels are strong in a vertical direction, but not so good laterally, meaning that any sideways swipe can cause problems. You'll know if your wheels need attention, as they'll suddenly start to rub on the brake pads on every revolution where they're bent out of shape. Get a wheelbuilder to straighten them up when things get bad.

Another common wheel problem occurs when the rim sidewalls wear down because the brake pads are scrubbing against them. The rubber brake pads hang onto the bits of grit in mud, and this makes the perfect material for grinding metal off the rim sidewall, leading to serious failure if you're not careful. On the trail, this can result in the rim sidewall splitting and the tire bulging off the rim, locking up the wheel. If this happens downhill, at speed, and under braking, you don't have to think too hard to imagine what the consequences might be. Check for rim wear, and replace the rims before the braking surfaces go concave. Don't confuse rim wear with rims that have a concave section from new, or rims that have a braking ridge on them, which might give you cause for alarm.

FITTING A NEW TIRE

1 Deflate the inner tube by pressing the valve in with your finger, then work the tire bead loose by pushing it into the center of the rim.

2 Put a tire lever under the tire bead and lever it outwards, popping the bead over the edge of the rim.

3 Push a second tire lever around the rim to loosen more of the tire. Remove the tire from the rim, simply by pulling it off, then remove the inner tube.

4 Fit one bead of the new tire to the rim. If the tire is front or rear specific, check that you've got the right tire, and ensure that the direction arrows on the tire are correct.

5 Fit the inner tube, securing it with the valve-nut if needed.

6 Relocate the bead on the rim, working around. Try to get the tire on without using the levers. They could rip or tear the tube.

7 Finally, pump the tire up to the correct pressure. Pumps are available with built-in pressure gauges.

Adjusting the gears

Using a somewhat archaic system of cables pulling sprung parallelograms, mountain bike gears work surprisingly well, despite not having changed a great deal since their inception over seventy years ago.

Problems are mostly down to low cable tension, caused by stretching under prolonged use. If the cable tension's wrong then the derailleur isn't in the right place and the gears won't shift to the correct cog. Slack cables can be spotted as they hang loose when the bike is shifted to its smallest cogs. Cables should be just tight when in this position.

RUST AND CORROSION

Another problem is gunged- or rusted-up cables. Gear systems need a low-friction cable run. Without this, gears are hard to shift to larger cogs, or even to smaller cogs, because the outer cables housings 'hang on' to the inner cable, stopping the derailleur dropping to the smaller cogs. This is a particular problem on the last piece of cable running into the rear derailleur (because of the tight bend) and on the outer cable housing where the cable comes out of the shifter. When cables are gunged-up, you can disassemble the system, re-lube them and re-install them. But the best thing to do is to replace either the whole gear cable set, or the specific bit of gunged-up cable. Outer cables get gritty beyond repair. Inner cables *can* be cleaned and reused, but the gear cable is usually so ragged at the end that this isn't possible, so if you replace outer cable housing, replace the inner cable as well.

GEAR ADJUSTMENT: REAR DERAILLEUR

1 Shift the front derailleur so the bike is in the middle chainring. Shift the rear derailleur so that the bike is in the smallest cog.

2 Wind the gear adjuster all the way in (fully clockwise).

3 Loosen the rear derailleur cable clamp and pull the cable through until it's tight, then tighten the cable clamp again.

4 Shift the rear shifter up one click, and then turn the cranks with the rear wheel off the ground.

5 If the chain doesn't move to the next biggest cog turn the adjuster on the rear derailleur half a turn, or until the gears shift.

6 If the chain jumps to the next highest cog wind the adjuster in a quarter turn and repeat until it stays on the right cog.

GEAR ADJUSTMENT: FRONT DERAILLEUR

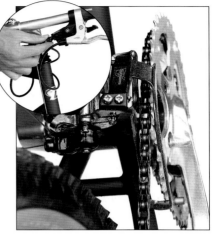

1 Shift the front derailleur so that the bike is in the middle chainring.

2 Shift the rear derailleur to the middle cog.

3 Use the cable adjuster at the shifter to pull the cable through until the chain is no longer rubbing on the derailleur.

CABLE REPLACEMENT

1 Shift the rear derailleur onto the smallest cog.

2 Release the cable from the rear derailleur cable clamp.

3 Cut the ragged part off the cable.

4 Pull the cable out of the derailleur, and through the cable housing.

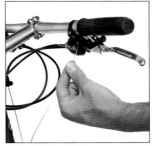

5 Replace the section of cable that's gritted up. Cut the cable to length and fit end caps.

6 Lubricate the outer cable housing, using a water repellent spray.

7 Fit a new cable. Feed the cable into the shifter, and through all the outer cable housing.

8 Stretch the cable, then follow the 'Gear Adjustment' details to set up the rear derailleur.

Suspension forks

If you don't spend time setting your suspension forks up properly, you might as well not use them at all. Forks that are too hard or too soft won't work through the bumps properly, which basically means that you're dragging a lot of extra weight around with no benefit.

MEASURING COMPRESSION

Suspension forks (and rear suspension systems, too) should compress a little when you sit on the bike. If they don't compress enough, the springs are set up too hard, and if they compress too easily, then you're going to use up all the available travel on small bumps.

1 Measure the distance between two points on the suspension fork.

2 Sit on the bike on a level surface, in a riding position. Have a friend measure the distance between the same two points.

3 Adjust the preload, or add or remove air to make the fork compress 1⁄6th of its travel (10mm for a 60mm fork).

ADJUSTING STIFFNESS

If the forks are far too hard or too soft, then it's necessary to change the stiffness of the springs.

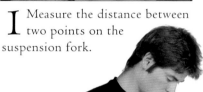

spring

elastomer

Some forks use elastomers as the springing medium – small pieces of foam rubber that provide a lightweight alternative to heavier steel springs. However, other forks use a combination of elastomers and springs to provide the bounce in the fork. Changing them is simple and doesn't require getting covered in oil or compressed air. Indeed, modern suspension forks are designed to be maintained by the home mechanic.

By removing the top caps with a socket wrench, you will be able to access the elastomers or spring units. Elastomers are usually contained on a skewer or clipped together with plastic plugs. Change one of the elastomers for a harder or softer rubber, depending on your requirement. Spring stops can be changed to either longer or shorter units.

Adjusting the setup

If you're uncomfortable on your bike, then it's worth looking at the position of your saddle and handlebars before you start thinking about buying a new one.

SADDLE AND SEATPOST

Most modern mountain bikes have seatposts that allow infinite adjustment, raising or lowering the nose of the saddle to position it just right for you. Additionally, the saddle can be moved forwards or backwards, to alter your position relative to the bottom bracket and handlebars.

1 Loosen the clamp bolt under the rear of the saddle and slide saddle to the new position.

2 You will be able to adjust the position either up or down, or forwards and backwards.

TWIN-BOLT SEATPOST CLAMP

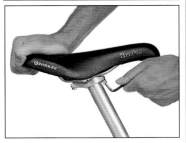

Some seatposts have twin-bolt clamps. By tightening or loosening opposing bolts you will be able to pull the saddle to the right position.

3 Clamp up the bolts securely, checking that the saddle doesn't move.

STEM HEIGHT

It is only possible to adjust the height of your stem if you have the older type of threaded headset. Aheadset stems clamp in place on the bike, and the only way of changing the position of your handlebars is to buy a new stem with a different amount of 'rise'.

1 Loosen the allen bolt in the top of the stem.

2 Tap the top of the allen bolt with a bit of wood to loosen the clamp inside the stem.

3 Gripping the front wheel between your knees, raise the stem, but not past the 'Max Height' mark, and tighten the allen bolt.

CHAPTER SIX

World biking

Bored with backyard biking and fancy moving to some real terrain? Well, there's nothing to stop you simply packing up your bike and bags and heading off to a mountain wilderness for a week or two. If you prefer a slightly easier option, there's a growing breed of enthusiast-led holiday companies whose popularity is catching on fast. This chapter is just the tip of the iceberg. It includes a selection of mountain bike holiday destinations that we've sampled and enjoyed and that should really inspire you to get up and go. Our destinations are graded, from a relaxed trip to historic French Normandy, to the high Alpine thrills of Chamonix and a long-distance tour in New Zealand — with plenty of other suggestions in between. Everyone should find something here.

Easy biking

Not everyone wants the crash-and-burn thrills of big mountains and the gnarly single-track challenges that the expert mountain biker devours. There are plenty of opportunities around the world for easy-going jaunts into beautiful countryside. Add a smattering of local history, good company and fine food and you've discovered some of the main reasons why people start mountain biking and never want to stop.

If you regard yourself as an easy-grade rider, you could choose to focus your mountain bike holiday on almost anywhere in the modern world. A system of trails or minor roads linking urban centers and amenities is really the only prerequisite. The extensive trail net of Northern Europe could be the ideal place to start.

THE NORMANDY EXPERIENCE

The area we visited, Haut Maine et Pail, is a relatively undiscovered area of heavily wooded, ridged hills that were formed during the great upheavals of the Armorican uplands. Today these parts lie within the Regional National Park of Normandy-Maine. The area is reached in about an hour and a half's drive from the English Channel port of Caen.

BEING THERE

Cycling around this area will introduce you to a whole new world of biking. There are some real surprises in store from this history-packed region. The backwaters of rural Normandy provided the cavalry for William the Conqueror to make his historic move on the English coast in 1066, and fortresses and feudal villages still litter the countryside. You'll find that some of them have even been converted into excellent food establishments. Normandy is the perfect spot for the gourmet mountain biker to enjoy 'Le Weekend' – two or three days of trail-blazing, feasting on the hidden culinary and scenic treats of Normandy and enjoying the welcoming Gallic culture.

Meandering through picturesque, thickly forested hills of ancient beech and oak in the Bocage Ornais region (also known as Swiss Normandy), our guide pointed out the 'Grande Route' and 'Petite Route' (GR & PR)

HISTORY LESSON
Some of the historic fortresses that litter the countryside have been converted into excellent restaurants and lodgings for the mountain biker.

SINGLE-TRACK HEAVEN
Lines of enticing trails disappear into the dark hearts of tree- and rock-swathed valleys.

signs on the trees. These marked the lines of enticing trails that disappeared into the dark hearts of tree- and rock-swathed valleys. This was superb. Our pre-conceived image of Normandy was based around flat battlefields, the Bayeux Tapestry and Calvados brandy. No one had told us about the MTB routes.

As the terrain progressed from firm farm tracks and leafy lanes into deep, dark forest and twisty single-track, there were plenty of opportunities for both showing off and learning. The more playful members of the group were soon more than happy to share their rock-hopping skills with the beginners amongst us.

The terrain rose, almost imperceptibly, as we followed Grande Route links through the rolling National Park forest of Ecouvres, where ancient woodland merges with managed evergreens. Occasionally-tough fire-trail climbs up the tree lines were rewarded with swoops down rocky valley folds. These folds build slowly toward a 1300 ft (400 m) bumpy forest spine — and a breathtaking outlook over Normandy, Brittany and the distant coastline. We were close to the summit of the Mont Des Avaloirs. At 1370 ft (417 m), this is the highest point in northwest France; not exactly a mountain, but a little more than we had expected.

We donned windproof shells to shun the inevitable chill-rush that would accompany the dramatic descent. Warnings of rocky, skittish

terrain ahead topped up the thrill factor as we fixed our eyes on the plunging grassy trail-line.

It was then that we hit some muddy single-track. This was the most technically demanding part so far. Steep, rocky drops through tiny streams provided a challenge as we all made several attempts to get across. The beginners of the group tackled stuff they'd only ever seen in magazine pictures and they were loving every minute of it – learning fast and pushing their limits way beyond earlier expectations.

WHY HAUT MAINE ET PAIL?

The well-marked Grande Route and Petite Route trails that criss-cross this area are almost all open to MTBs (it will be obvious if they're not). There are about 1240 miles (2000 km) of way-marked trails in the whole National Park area and their use is actively encouraged by local tourist offices. Detailed maps can be obtained at town offices.

Accommodation is cheap and is commonly in the form of a Gite d'etape or a Chambre d'hôte (bed & breakfast). A traditional Gite is a country house or converted farmhouse with room or dormitory accommodation. Gites, b-and-bs and the many campsites in the area are all graded. Biking holidays in Normandy are not really weather-dependent, but the trails are usually drier between April and September.

A TRANQUIL SCENE
In Normandy, you can ride, hear about the amazing history of the region or simply absorb the rural tranquillity.

Island biking

For warm-weather, year-round riding, you can't go far wrong heading for one of the many islands off the extensive Mediterranean coastline. Most are well served by major airlines and seasonal tourism and the riding is generally easy-access, if not very well signposted. But there are wonderful islands in other spots, too.

There are great island highlights all over the world. These include a mass of tiny Greek islands, but check maps before you go — some of them are too small to need a developed trail net. The Canary Islands, off the coast of Africa, are volcanic in character and offer all sorts of challenging terrain, from rocky goat tracks to big-scale, four wheel drive trails that link the surfaced roads. Tenerife and Fuerta Ventura are probably the most suitable islands for MTBs. Cyprus, Ibiza, Corsica, Sardinia and Majorca are all good holiday spots for a mix of beach and MTB activity.

THE GREEK ISLE OF LEFKAS

Lefkas lies to the west of Greece. It's actually linked to the mainland by a long, narrow causeway. The longest part of the island is 34 miles (55 km) and the highest point is the 3742 ft (1141 m) Mount Stavrota. The population is about 30,000. Most visitors fly in to the military airport near Vonitsa, which is only open in season, but it is still possible to get there out of season by flying to Corfu or Athens. There are plenty of hotels, bed-and-breakfasts, rooms to rent, and a fair amount of campsites.

CAR-LESS TRAILS
Once you're off the coast, many Lefkas roads are too rough for cars, but access for bikes is almost unlimited.

BEING THERE

Agias Donatos was a little white church that sat and beckoned on the 3280 ft (1000 m) peak that topped the rolling hills rising from the Lefkas coast. It had beckoned since arrival and we all knew that everything else was leading up to a grand last-day ascent, which would probably take up to four hours for the less accomplished members of the group. There was no rush. In this part of Greece, there's more than enough hardcore riding for the adrenaline addicts. For the first-timers, the reluctant partners and those who simply want to cruise, there are easy trails through the olive groves and meanderings along the coast. And, when it all gets too much, there's always the beach.

The days developed a highly enjoyable pattern — morning ride, lazy lunch, an afternoon swim and doze on the beach before dinner at the local taverna — but there's something about mountain biking that dictates that the best days are always the excessive ones. From day one, talk centerd on the last day's ride to the white church. They told us that it's impossible

RACEY TRAILS (*above*)
There are plenty of opportunities on Lefkas for the hardcore crew to race ahead, then meet up with the others at the next village for coffee and cakes.

MASSIVE DESCENTS (*right*)
We were told that the often terrifying descent went on and on.

in the height of summer, with temperatures reaching 113 °F. They told us that there was a stretch of single-track up there that made even goat herds turn back, and that the terrifying descent went on for 20 miles (30 km)... The legend grew and, as with all the best rides, we knew that the myth was simply all the memorable parts from everyone's experiences rolled into one, with a spicy touch of imaginative fiction.

There are certainly sections of trail on Lefkas that are not for the faint-hearted but, where the challenge reaches extremes, there is always a soft option. Our group numbered twelve on the most enthusiastic days. We planned routes to allow fitter riders to hammer on ahead to the next

village, spring, or junction, while the less obsessed stopped to admire views, have a break or take a ride in the support Jeep. Having a volunteer to drive the Jeep every day was a real bonus.

WHY LEFKAS?

One of the nicest things about Lefkas is its massive variety of terrain and relaxed atmosphere. For the real MTB enthusiast, there's everything you could want, but there's just as much for novices. Maps are not detailed, so you would be better off going with an organized group. Temperatures vary between 77 °F at the season's limits to 113 °F in summer sun. There's very little rain but, when it comes, you get filthy and simply steam dry. The tourist season is 'closed' between mid-October and April (when restaurants and bars are shut).

Lefkas is a mountainous island, where most of the towns are on the coastal roads. Small villages and organized agriculture are dotted around the mountain roads but, once you're off the coast, there's very little traffic and many roads are too rough for cars. Access for bikes is almost unlimited, with a large network of goatherding trails, forest tracks and link routes between the paved sections.

RELAXING
One of the best things about Lefkas is its massive variety of terrain and relaxed atmosphere.

'Real' mountain biking

Of course, if you want to take your bike and your body to the limits and back, you'll have to go to some real mountains. Any mountain range that lies close to civilization, and many that don't, will have trail networks criss-crossing valleys and passes.

The more commercialized mountain resorts, typically those devoted to skiing, will have lift systems that can take you and your bike up to the trailheads, where the more dramatic downhill rides begin. In the US and Canada, the mountain territories offer no end of pleasures for the mountain biker, from the radical trails of Vancouver to the MTB meccas of Durango, Big Bear and Mammoth Mountain. Europe's mountain resorts in the Alps, the Pyrenees and the Dolomites are now catering to mountain bikers in a big way. Their low-level trails are often marked and mapped for easy use, while the high-level trails leave the more independent mountain biker's spirit of adventure intact.

THE LURE OF CHAMONIX

Chamonix is about 45 miles (75 km) southeast of Geneva. It's 3280 ft (1000 m) above sea level, so don't expect total trail access after the first snowfalls. From the town, there is little immediate gravity-assisted riding – it's all on the looming valley sides and peaks. If you hate riding up hill, no matter – there's an extensive lift system to take you to the tops. Most lifts take bikes, but some close after the winter. Valley rides are often still accessible well after the first winter snow, so a combined snow and bike holiday is feasible in the early and late winter seasons. There's a wide choice of bed and breakfast places, lodges, hotels and campsites.

BEING THERE
After a hard morning's riding, we'd left the bikes locked up at the cable car pay booth to make space for the tour-bus hordes who mimicked our own inclination to head for the highest attainable point. No one should visit Chamonix without experiencing the view of Mont Blanc from the Aiguille du Midi. Our original plan, to ride back down, was baulked by a lift

HARDCORE
There's plenty of riding at Chamonix for adrenaline freaks.

attendant – but this turned out to be the right move. The café perching perilously on the snowy slopes of the Aiguille du Midi sold the most costly cup of coffee in the Chamonix Valley. But it also offered other wonders – at 12,601 ft (3842 m) above sea level, this was the closest to the sun we'd been without the protection of a reclining seat and safety instructions. The combination of thin air and the exhilarating exhaustion of a week's hard Alpine mountain biking conspired to make us feel as impressed as we could be by the serene majesty of this dream panorama.

I aimed the binoculars at the pearly domes that build toward the summit of Europe's highest peak. My eyes welcomed a refuge from the midday glare as I twiddled the focus dial to pick up human chains cramponing ever-upward. Two of our ride colleagues were among them, experiencing the altitude-induced weariness that makes ordinary MTB racing feel as easy as

running for a bus. Their bikes were evenly distributed between four others for the thirteen-hour ascent. They had no idea whether they'd be the first to ride an MTB on the 15766 ft (4807 m) summit of Mont Blanc, but it seemed like a good idea at the time.

The draw of the Alps has held me since my first attempt to ride to 100 summits in a month. There's something about Chamonix that exemplifies perfectly the human link with the drama, spirit and colossal power of the mountains. It seems fitting that a mountain resort should cower in a valley, dominated by the looming presence of active geography. The perpetually shifting glaciers and cycle of snow-to-water, plus the occasional forest-mowing avalanche, all stress the frailty of the human dimension – but it's this frailty that makes any attempt at nature-conquering activities that much more consuming.

Chamonix has become an

MTB PARADISE
Some of the best rides are hidden, and they cover every conceivable terrain challenge.

Alpine center for skiers, climbers, hill walkers, paragliders, canyoners, mountain bikers and just about anyone who can appreciate its uniquely clear climate and landscape.

Playing in mountains demands a real respect for both the power and fragility of the environment. Over-use of nature's resources is an issue in Chamonix and the use of some MTB trails is not officially authorized during July and August. For the rest of the spring, summer and autumn, it's a mountain biker's paradise, and even in those two peak months, there's enough to keep even the most obsessed rider happy.

The best rides are hidden, and they cover every conceivable terrain challenge – from casual pottering along the valley riverside to vein-stretching climbs and

rocky-horror descents, switchback single-tracks and some of the best graded trails you'll find anywhere. The Chamonix Office du Tourisme has a map that grades all authorized trails as green, blue, red or black (ski piste system), but local knowledge unveils a further myriad of superb trails.

WHY CHAMONIX?

If you go for a week or two, you'll have more than enough time to explore all the mapped trails in the valley (maps are free from the Office du Tourisme in Chamonix) and, for the endurance freaks, to plot a route for a three-countries circumnavigation of Mont Blanc. As long as you don't mind taking in several enormous climbs, you can head upward and eastward out of the top end of the valley into Switzerland, and then tack west into Italy before returning, via three cols that top 8200 ft (2500 m), into France. It's not an undertaking for the faint-hearted. You'll need full mountain survival kit and you'll have to be prepared to push and carry in places. It's been done in one long summer's day, and a 90 mile (150 km) route can be planned to include long stretches of paved road, but even strong riders would be wise to allow for at least two overnight stops.

The holiday season in Chamonix is from May to October. Warm, sunny days abound in season, but be prepared for big changes higher up.

MONT BLANC CIRCUMNAVIGATION
This is not an undertaking for the faint-hearted, but it's a truly superb MTB experience.

Theme park biking

Many mountain resorts are taking their mountain bike visitors seriously these days. Marked trails and maps can make days out far easier to plan, and some resorts are color-coding the trails in the same way as ski pistes — green for easy; blue for easy but getting hilly; red for advanced; black for very experienced only.

In the US, Durango, Mammoth Mountain and Vail all have well-marked trails and, although it's impossible to generalize about mountain biking in the US, there are many other areas starting to take up the MTB tourist challenge.

Many places have their highlights, but the ones that are really talked about tend to be those that offer the most to short-term visitors. Marin County, the 'birthplace' of the MTB, has been a mecca for a long time, but the reality is that the trails are restricted these days. Team up with a local, however, and you will still discover the reasons for its fame. Moab, the home of the infamous slick rock, has this and a great deal more to offer besides. Try the White Rim Tour or just go exploring with a trail map. There's much more to it than rock.

WINTER PARK RESORT, COLORADO

Winter Park is close enough to Denver to fly into the city in the morning and be riding in the afternoon (it's just over an hour's drive). If you're in Denver with a day or two to spare, rent a car or catch a Greyhound bus and head for the Park. There's an Amtrak train service to Winter Park twice a day with a bus to the resort from the train station. The Zephyr — a high-speed chairlift up to the top — will take you and your bike to the Sunspot café all day long (if you're over 70, it's free!). It runs every day from mid-June until early September, and on weekends in September. You can rent bikes in Winter Park if you don't want to bring your own. The weather is changeable, as with any location at altitude, so be prepared with your clothing. It's generally good in the summer months, when you can usually just show up and book into a motel. That's the best way if you're not sure how long you'll be staying.

Just to put you even more in the picture, on one side of Denver you have the Colorado Rockies, an imposing group of sharp ranges. On

EXCELLENT FACILITIES
Follow the marked trails or just go exploring with a trail map.

the other side you have nothing. Well, not exactly nothing. It's just that the plains that stretch from those foothills to the East Coast, about 2,000 miles (3,000 km) away, are a mountain biker's idea of nothing. So the only thing a self-respecting mountain biker can do when arriving in Denver is head west. It's just a short drive from Denver to a huge variety of resorts and top MTB destinations, all vying for the tourist buck. There's glitzy Aspen and Vail, remote Durango, tiny Crested Butte... all good destinations for mountain bikers. Where do you begin? Winter Park is as good a place as any, and a great deal better than most. If there is now a new concept of an MTB theme park, it's places like this that spawned the concept in the first place.

BEING THERE

You'll feel the altitude in Winter Park. It's not debilitating, but you'll be breathing like a novice diver for a while. The Winter Park base camp is at 9000 ft (2700 m); the top of the mountain is at 10,700 ft (3,200 m), and the top is where all the fun starts. With the Zephyr chairlift to take you back up whenever you want, you can ride single-track downhill for pretty much the whole day.

If you prefer to earn your downhill miles, you can either ride up the service road to the summit or take the more challenging single-track. The only problem with the single-track up is that you have to contend with the

bikers coming down. And it's not always that easy! The theory is that bikers coming down give way to those going up, but when you're shredding a gnarly section of first-class single-track, stopping isn't always your greatest priority. On the way down you do need to watch for hikers, but we were amazed at how few we came across, and how friendly they were.

A particularly great thing about Winter Park is the 'mountain host' system, a scheme that's been carried over successfully from the ski season. The summer hosts do two organized tours per day, meeting at the Lodge (by the Sunspot) and taking anyone who wants to go out trail-blazing. It's a loosely-run thing, depending on the size and ability of the group. When not guiding a specific group, their job is to ride the trails, meet people and offer help and advice. They're as likely to talk about the vegetation, wildlife

FOREST SINGLE-TRACK
There are fairly easy descents, with fun single-track going in and out of the evergreen and aspen forests.

and geography as trail etiquette and riding tips. They'll also point out radical trails to more experienced riders. If there are mishaps, help is never far away. It's rare to see this sort of dedication toward promoting mountain biking as a regular activity at a resort.

If you follow the Long trail all the way to the base, it's a fairly easy descent, with fun single-track going in and out of evergreen and aspen forests. Of course, the faster you go, the less easy it becomes. Starting the day climbing from Sunspot to the higher elevations, you soon wind up in silvery aspen groves and deep evergreen forests, crossing streams and cruising through meadows, and all the while being seduced by the subtly

changing panorama of the front range of the Colorado Rockies.

At slow speeds, the green trails are easy enough for beginners to handle, but if you increase the pace even these provide a buzz. Lower Arapahoe has narrow sections of single-track twisting through trees and punctuated by steep switchbacks, although they're clearly marked with big yellow 'Caution' signs. Bobbing and weaving, we chased each other down the mountain until our arms ached from braking. Grinning from ear to ear, we just had to go back up and do it again.

WHY WINTER PARK?

Winter Park is a great place for mountain bikers. Some 45 miles (72 km) of single-track snakes around the Winter Park Mountain, and it's all marked, mapped, superbly maintained and graded according to degree of difficulty. The trail maps work just like ski maps, and they're marked on the ground, so they're easy to follow. The fun doesn't stop there either. Fraser Valley, where the resort is located, has almost 600 miles (1,000 km) of manicured trails just waiting for you. The valley's trail types vary enormously, from wide, easy-for-beginners dirt roads to radical, technical single-track. It would take for ever to explore all these options. The Winter Park bike season starts as soon as the ski season finishes.

THAT'S WHERE WE CAME FROM
Grinning from ear to ear, we just had to go back and do it again.

Exotic biking

These days, there are many organized mountain bike tours to the African and Asian continents. Particular highlights are the Atlas mountains in Morocco and parts of South Africa, Kenya, Tanzania and Nepal. Get to know as much as you can about these countries before you visit. Ask about visas, politics, food, drink, language and customs.

The southern hemisphere can often appear more easily accessible for the independent traveller. Australia is too massive to generalize about, but there are some true MTB highlights in New South Wales, Queensland and Victoria. If you're looking for somewhere more out of the way, try the islands of Fiji. Most areas are very welcoming and, with the right maps, you can find some superb trails between villages. New Zealand is a great place to spend time biking. Mix road with off-road and you could tour the whole of the South Island in a month or two.

ON THE LONG TRAIL IN NEW ZEALAND

If you want to get a real taste for riding through the back country of the South Island, try the Molesworth Track that links Blenhein with Hanmer Springs. It's a tough two- to three-day (90 mile/150 km) haul across one of New Zealand's biggest cattle farms, on tracks that are only open to motorized vehicles for a couple of months a year. You'll need to be self-sufficient; there are no stores, and very few houses, en route.

If you're a single-track fan, you can't go far wrong by heading for Rotorua on the North Island. This is a region of great significance to the Maori population. It's a hyperactive volcanic area too; MTB route maps and guided trips

COASTAL CRUISING
New Zealand offers quiet roads that at times feel more like off-road.

will take you to all the special places, but don't leave before you've checked out the MTB routes in the Whakarewarewa Forest.

BEING THERE

Whakarewarewa. Long before you've learned how to say it properly, you'll be revelling in its comprehensive web of purpose-built single-track. The forest of Whakarewarewa is a magical place. The trails are carved from the earth in a way that feels somehow organic, as though the old forest grew that way. Reading this South Island terrain well will make you a true mountain biker. As you swing through the corkscrewed twists and turns, with banked corners and tree chicane options for the tricksters among you, you catch glimpses of color flashing through the trees from the riders following on, two, three or more minutes behind. It really is very rare to come across this sort of trail intensity. You're in a world of your own as soon as you enter the net, but you're never more than a stone's throw from the place where you started. Wonderful.

On South Island, the mountains beckon from Blenheim, but they beckon gently. This will be a long day. A morning of steady riding takes you from pavement to trail, over the first range of hills and away from the few motorized vehicles that venture this far. A wide but twisting descent across smooth-baked dirt drops down to the Molesworth track proper. Think carefully about those houses. Do you have enough food and water? Is your bike sound? In an hour or so, you'll be on dirt and you may not see another soul until

the warden at the camp eight hours later.

We were tired, hungry and covered in thick dust, which formed into ridges where the sweat gathered. Two days of riding close to our physical limits, across what felt like wilderness to pampered city dwellers like us, had taken its toll, but the trail now started to drop. We stopped to look at map contours. It was time to rejoice. Pushing hunger and tiredness to the back of our minds, we plummeted at the speed of light down a trail that seemed to be carved from solid rock toward Hamner Springs. Houses appeared, some with lawns. We'd only spent two days away from civilization, but it felt great to be back.

WHY NEW ZEALAND?

Most cycle tourists visit the South Island of New Zealand, because the roads are quieter and the scenery is more mountainous. A mountain bike is a better option than a road bike here because, although there are surfaced roads linking urban

MOLESWORTH TRACK

A morning of steady riding takes you over the first hill range, then down to the trail that leads you 90 miles (150 km) across one of New Zealand's biggest cattle farms.

areas, the most spectacular touring roads are the rough-surfaced cross-country links.

Most New Zealand cities have an active MTB scene. Just call into a local bike shop to find out what an area offers. The best time to go cycle touring in New Zealand is just before the end of their summer, starting around early March. Because the schools go back then, there is less traffic on the roads, and fewer hikers off-road. The best weather, however, is before then, when the northern hemisphere is experiencing winter. Remember that, whatever the time of year, you can expect some wet weather if you travel down the west coast of the South Island. But pick your spot well, and you'll be in bikers' paradise.

CHAPTER SEVEN

In competition

Mountain biking is a race-led sport. Manufacturers use racers, races and racing to promote and develop the sport — as a result, racing mountain bikes has become a popular pastime for many riders. Even though mountain bike racing is now an Olympic sport, you don't have to be a professional rider to take part. As well as world-class events happening in many countries around the globe, there are a variety of smaller local events that cater for the first-time and intermediate racers. There are several different types of event that you and your bike can enter. Many riders see multi-lap cross-country racing as the one-and-only discipline, but there are other events — such as the increasingly popular (and dangerous) downhill, dual slalom, trials, trailquest and ultra-distance events.

Cross-country racing

For many riders, the cross-country race is the ultimate celebration of the efficiency partnership between body and bike. Top cross-country racers are among the world's fittest athletes, but the beauty of MTB racing is that anyone can try it. In most cases, you simply show up, pay a fee, sign a piece of paper and go to the start line.

Generally, a cross-country mountain bike race will be raced on a 4-6 mile (6½-9½ km) circuit. The racers don't all compete in the same race; they are split into age and ability classes. Different classes will complete between one and six laps of the course, with perhaps two or three classes running on the course at the same time. The courses will form a loop that covers different types of trail, including at least one major climb, a technical section and a downhill. Race organizers try to avoid the mountain bike rider's idea of heaven – single track. This is because it doesn't offer the chance to pass easily, leading to crashes when riders try to make headway regardless of whether they can do so safely.

It's not necessary to be a top-class athlete to compete at this level. Most races have a 'fun' or 'beginner' class, where riders who aren't interested in being at the top of their sport can battle it out in a slightly more lighthearted manner than some of their fellow competitors. Fun races are the places where people can have a good time, riding a great course with fellow bikers. Some people even turn up in costume!

The Sport class forms the real grass roots of the sport, populated by riders who may train one or two days a week, and could be considered 'serious' cyclists. Sport riders will typically ride around 18-22 miles (29-35 km) in a race.

The next class up is termed 'Expert', and consists of riders who have consistently placed well

FAST START
Riders go out hard to get a lead as soon as possible.

in Sports class races. They will have either decided to take the greater challenge of racing Expert class, or have been promoted by the mountain bike racing governing body to ride the course distance of around 25 miles (40 km). Many countries run a points scheme, where racers competing at sanctioned races win points based on their finish positions. If they exceed a certain amount of points in a particular year, they will be promoted to a higher ability category.

The highest level class is Pro/Elite. These are the racers who race for a living and are paid by their sponsors. A Pro rider will ride for four or five days each week, and compete all year round, perhaps dabbling occasionally in cyclo-cross and road racing. A typical Pro level race distance is around 30 miles (48 km).

THE RACE ITSELF

Cross-country races have a mass start, with the field separated into separate categories. The fastest riders set off first. In a Pro level race, the Pro riders go first, and the race organizers may well run the Expert riders two minutes behind them. A Sports race will usually have the whole circuit to itself, as that class has the largest number of entrants.

Mountain bike racers ride hard, right from the word go. Riders coming from road-race backgrounds are more used to races building in speed over the first quarter of the course, with the pace picking up towards the end. Mountain bike races are almost the complete opposite, with riders going out hard to get a lead as fast as possible. Having no

other riders in front of you is an advantage as it means no hold-ups in difficult sections. As the race progresses, riders often end up riding on their own, with other riders as much as a couple of minutes ahead of or behind them. It's certainly quite rare for any tactics, drafting (taking pace from another rider) or teamwork to take place, though on shorter courses this can come into play.

No technical assistance is allowed during the race. Any mechanical problems that may arise

VARIETY RULES
Races take in every conceivable terrain type, from tough climbs to radical descents and big forest trails.

must be fixed by the riders themselves, including flats and broken equipment. The only outside help allowed is the supply of food and drink to riders by helpers; vital in a race that may last up to four hours. It's as simple as that. And the winner is the first rider over the line in each specific class.

Downhill competitions

Downhill racing is now almost a completely separate sport to cross-country, with very few riders competing seriously in both. The best downhillers will compete on a potent mix of nerve, incredible skill, a surprisingly high level of all-round fitness and a boost of adrenaline that would make many people shake like a leaf.

This is one of the up-and-coming 'gravity sports' in mountain biking. Downhilling has always been a strong part of mountain biking. It's so much fun and is a real test of skill, rather than total aerobic fitness. That's not to say that downhillers are unfit. Their strength tends to lie in their ability to pound the pedals hard for around five minutes, but certainly no more. As this is a very different sort of fitness to that required for cross-country racing, downhilling has its own set of riders who compete only in downhill races. Some cross-country riders compete to high levels in both events, but they are the exception rather than the rule.

Downhill courses obviously go downhill, but it's not all a sheer, plunging-off-the-side-of-a-cliff type of downhill. Lumps, jumps and bumps are all there too, either naturally or artificially created to give something to separate out the really great bike handlers.

Downhilling is a highly technical sport, both in terms of the skills required to succeed and the level of equipment needed. As the courses have developed in severity, the type of equipment used has changed. A few years ago, some riders were riding downhills competitively on fully rigid bikes with stock equipment – exactly the same set-up that they would race in cross-country events.

Nowadays, world-class downhilling pretty much demands full suspension, with 6 to 8 in (15 to 20 cm) of wheel travel, disc brakes and flat resistant tires – the average downhill bike now looks like a motorbike without an engine.

THE RACE ITSELF

Downhilling is a time-trial. Riders are usually seeded in qualifying runs before the main race. More often than not, it's a one-run, do-or-die race. Any mistakes, mechanical failures, flats or whatever are insignificant – you get one run down the hill to post your time, and that's that. It might seem a pretty tough way to decide a race, but it means simply that the bike stays together, the rider doesn't crash – and the fastest person wins.

BIG TERRAIN *(left)*
The world's best courses are inevitably set in some of the biggest mountain terrain, with courses plummeting down the slopes to the towns nestling in the vales below.

FULL THROTTLE *(right)*
Downhill racing is certainly not for the faint-hearted, even if your only a spectator.

Dual slalom

Dual slalom is the most intense form of racing, and certainly the most spectacular to watch. The thrills and spills come in equal measure and the courses tend to produce a constant stream of surprises from both rider and terrain.

Like an extreme downhill event, dual slalom pits two riders on twin-track, marked courses in an elimination style race to decide who goes through to the next round. Courses can vary in length from 20 seconds to two minutes or more, depending on the area of hillside available, the spacing between the gates and the whims of the organizer.

Slalom courses are like BMX tracks, unravelled and laid out down a hill. Berms (banked corners), jumps and ditches are all popular course features.

Riders that excel at dual slalom typically come from a BMX background, or from mountain bike downhill racing. However, the bikes used for dual slalom are quite different to those for downhill racing. Generally they're small and short with no rear suspension, to give the riders the speed and power they need to sprint out of corners hard. They're also light, so that they can be jumped easily, and have extremely powerful brakes, allowing riders to put off slowing down for as long as possible. Front suspension forks are also used, with high, wide, downhill-style handlebars.

THE RACE ITSELF

Riders start side-by-side on a start gate. When the gate drops, they sprint down the course, passing through gates before racing for the finish line. Race organizers always try to make both lanes of equal distance and hardness, but, inevitably, one will always be a favorite. Racers toss a coin to decide who takes which lane.

THE PROFESSIONALS *(right)*
Getting air is all part of the game in dual slalom.

INTENSE COMPETITION *(below)*
The shoulder-to-shoulder action that typifies dual slalom makes for high-intensity racing.

Trailquest

A new type of competitive mountain bike event is gaining popularity. Some people call it orienteering. Some people call it touring. The organizers call it Trailquest, and it's an event that appears to encompass all the ideals of MTB self-sufficiency and camaraderie.

While mountain biking is generally cross-country race led, the competition that is actually closest to the sort of riding most of us do is 'trailquest'. Gaining in popularity in many areas, this offers a different sort of competition that suits older riders with real mountain and outdoors experience. That said, there are many younger people taking part in these events. It's simply a very different form of mountain bike competition, and one that's going to grow over the years.

Exact details vary from event to event, but most trailquest races run roughly as follows. Competitors are given map reference points of checkpoints in a given area, say 30 miles by 30 miles (50 km by 50 km). Points are also allocated to these checkpoints, depending on their remoteness. Teams must ride around, visiting checkpoints and collecting points, and then (and this is the hard part) get back to the start within a given time, or face having points deducted for being late. Getting back early isn't a crime, but get back too early, and you've wasted time because it would have been possible to get more points.

Some events even include a

IDITASPORT
The ultimate super-marathon. Two days' riding across ice and snow.

remote overnight stop, which means that competitors not only have to get around the course, but they have to do it carrying all their equipment (and food) for an overnight stop as well.

Though this might all seem like incredibly hard work, it is possible to make a trailquest as hard as you want it to be. You don't have to rush around the four corners of the map to tick off all the difficult checkpoints, you can just ride from the start to the campsite via several tea shops if you like. This is what is now making trailquest events so popular. That, and the night-time bonfires and camaraderie.

THE POLARIS CHALLENGE
(left and right) Very popular in the UK, the Challenge combines map-reading skills wih fitness, fun and bike skills.

World class racing

As mountain bikes have reached the public 'en masse', an international competition circuit has grown up to cater for the needs of both riders and sponsors. Now top riders can earn decent salaries and TV is starting to dictate the rules.

Mountain bike racing is a worldwide event, with huge numbers of competitors coming from Europe, the US and Canada. The premier race series is the Grundig World Cup, consisting of downhill and cross-country events in ten locations around the globe. In 1996, these races were held as far apart as Quebec, Australia and Hawaii. The World Cup is divided into separate cross-country and downhill championships. In each event, the winner is decided over all the races, with competitors receiving points for the position they finish in every race. The rider with the best positions at the end of the series is the overall event champion. The World Cup is currently the only world-wide series, and is recognized as such by the world cycling governing body, the UCI.

As well as the World Cup, every country holds its own National Championships; there is also a European Championship and the annual World Championship. Both

WOMEN COMPETITORS
MTB racing is an open sport and the top women stars attract just as much attention as the men.

cross-country and downhill events feature at these races, but once again it's the on-the-day performance that counts.

Cross-country mountain biking was made an Olympic sport in 1996, and Italy's Paula Pezzo and Holland's Bart Bretjens were the first Olympic champions.

RIDING FOR A TEAM *(left)*
In the World Cup race series, sponsored teams look to buy in the top riders at the beginning of each season. You'll see the same jerseys cropping up over and over again.

PROFESSIONAL ABILITY *(right)*
It takes time, practice and an incredible amount of commitment to become a sponsored team rider. Even trials riders can get to earn some money with their skills.

Training for racing

Chapter Four covered aspects of getting in shape, but racing requires a degree of proper training to succeed, so the fitness aspect is worth a separate mention here. The amount of training required, and the regimentation of that training, depends largely on the level you want to reach, how fit you are naturally, and how dedicated you are to keeping to your training program.

There are many different approaches to training. Some are based on real on-the-bike work, others are based around more closely monitored turbo-training, where pulse monitors and cadence meters are used to give your body a very specific workout. To succeed at the highest levels of the sport, you need this latter type of finely tuned training, monitored carefully with the help of a professional coach.

Be aware that overtraining can be a very real, destructive problem. Overtrain, and you open yourself up to infection from colds and other infections. You will also find that you can't train properly because of tiredness, and your performance will start to worsen at every session. Rest is as important in a training regime as the exercise element. Ride hard every day, and you'll get fitter, for sure. But keep riding hard, and you'll become tired and your performance will decrease. Training properly means managing these rest and exercise timings in order to get the most from your body.

Training for a season of mountain bike racing really requires a three-stage plan. Throughout the early winter (October-January) you should concentrate on putting in long rides, but not at an especially high intensity level. Ensure that you're well rested during this time, and

TRAINING
Cross-training, or multi-discipline training, forms a major part of the mountain biker's pre-season plan. Gym work and running can be almost as important as the on-the-bike training.

perhaps spend time in the gym working on muscle groups that are under-developed.

From January until the start of the racing season, go for more specific training. The long rides shouldn't be abandoned, but shorter, harder rides should be included in the training programs – rides that emulate the kind of efforts that are likely to be involved in cross-country racing.

As the start of the season approaches (around the end of March in most countries), you should have built up the more intense part of the training, before resting for several days prior to your first competition.

During the race season, it's possible to ride every weekend, at race pace. And, without a doubt, the best training for racing is racing itself. Again, the importance of rest can't be overstressed. Without it, you'll run out of energy mid-season, and possibly succumb to injuries and the 'started too fast' gossip at the race site.

RACING FOOD

You'll expend far more energy in the two or three intense hours of a race than you would in a whole day of 'regular' riding. So the food you eat before and during a race is very important. The common analogy of the body as an engine is a perfect one here. Putting in either the wrong sort of fuel, not enough fuel, or fuel with bits of grit in it (keep with me on this one) will make the engine work badly.

To perform properly in a race, your body often needs energy from two sources. One is the carbohydrates that you've loaded up with over the days before the race – energy from this source only really comes into play with races of over an hour. Up until that point, your body is running on the energy from the food that you've just eaten. That's why it's so important to fuel yourself up properly before a ride. There are also a really wide variety of fitness foods available that are specially designed to be absorbed by your body as efficiently as possible.

What you drink can also make a difference to how well you perform, and you can purchase either carbohydrate- or mineral-

EATING

Bananas, energy bars, perhaps even chocolate. When you eat carbohydrates, they convert to energy. Always eat plenty before during and after a ride.

DRINKING

Some riders prefer to get all of their food energy from carbohydrate-loaded drinks. Even if you just drink water, drink lots of it. Dehydration is often the competitive mountain biker's downfall.

replacement drinks that keep your body at the right level of hydration. Without drinking enough, you'll deplete your energy supplies further, as your body won't be able to dig into its reserves efficiently.

Many books have been written on good diets for sports, and it's worth looking at them, and talking to other racers if you're interested in furthering your performance. They can make a real difference to your riding, especially over longer rides, when you can start to flag after 10 or so miles (15 kilometres).

Your first race

As we've said, mountain bike racing can be a very high-level sport, but for a first-time racer, there's no reason to worry too much. Racing isn't nearly as hard as the hype makes it out to be, and is usually not that far removed from simply riding around for a couple of hours with friends or hammering across town on a shorter sprint.

Use a pulse meter, use a turbo trainer, do whatever you like, but don't lose sight of why you're doing all this. If you can hammer hard for an hour or so, then you can race. A race is just a fast ride around a course with some other riders for an hour or two. Nothing more. The best riders will go eyeballs-out for the whole distance, but no one is going to complain or laugh if you have to stop for a breather at the top of all the hills. You won't win if you do this, but you'll finish, and they'll be plenty of other people doing it, too.

BIKE SELECTION

Racing at the highest level requires bikes that weigh less than your front wheel. And a lighter bike is definitely an easier and faster one to ride. But it's not essential, and a heavy bike is a great excuse for why people are coming past you on that tough climb! There's no 'legal' minimum standard of bike for racing. Basically, if it will take you around the rides that you do

START OF THE RACE

Get a reasonable place on the start line. The start is important. But don't line up at the front if you're among riders who are obviously far faster than you, even if it's just a fun race.

at the weekend without parts dropping off or bending, then it'll be fine for racing.

LET'S GO!

To get into the race scene, turn to the race calendar or news sections of your favorite magazine. Drop into the leading local shops and ask about nearby races. Stop likely-looking mountain bikers on the trails and enquire.

Races are divided into two groups: national and local. Many

mountain bikers choose to start racing at small local races before testing themselves on the national scene. That's fine. Local races offer a good place to get your feet wet without having to dive right in. If you've got the chance to try a national race without driving for too many hours to get there, then give it a go. National races have better facilities, more experienced organizers and more people to talk to. Their entry fees are higher and the standard of the riders may well

be better, but as you're only interested in hammering yourself at this stage, it's not a problem. Local races do usually give you the option of just showing up and entering, something that is rarely possible at the national level. Most national races require pre-registration anything up to three weeks before the event.

EXTRA GOODIES

To ensure a successful race, you need to pack more than just you and your bike. Take enough clothing to prepare you for a variety of weather conditions. Because you should be riding rapidly and not standing around too much, you can usually race in clothing that would be far too cold for a normal ride. The most you should need at any race is shorts, summer tights, short-sleeved jersey and long-sleeved jersey. Throw in a

lightweight shell top (like a Pertex) in case of torrential rain.

Take along a couple of spare water bottles so that your assistant (don't forget to pack one of these) can pass them up to you on each lap. Some races will have a drinks station.

It is a good idea to take spare parts, along with tools. Though your bike may be perfectly set up when you put it in the car, travelling often makes something work loose. Take a moderate amount of tools, and also take a spare tube and a pump, packing them on your bike so that you can get at them if need be.

Before you zip up the race holdall, remember that you're probably going to be finishing your race cold, wet and muddy. Throw in a bucket, sponge and towel as there's practically no chance that there will be showers in the field that the race is being held in!

THE RACE ITSELF

Cross-Country: Always try to get a good start, but this doesn't mean getting yourself into the thick of the action. Pick a place at the side of the starting area, and then, when the inevitable post-start pileup happens, you can ride round the action. Riding hard for the first ten minutes or so lets you get ahead of the real stragglers, then be prepared to settle into a fast pace and hold it for as long as possible.

Downhill and Dual Slalom: Make sure you get as much practice on

MAP READING
This is a basic requirement of Trailquest so be sure you know what you're doing.

the course as you can, but don't ride a thing until you've walked the course and checked out all the likely obstacles. Watch other riders' lines on the course, and try to see what they're doing through a particular section. When you start riding the course, don't go flat out on your first run, but take your time, building your speed up over successive runs until you attempt one at race-pace. On the run itself, concentrate on doing what you did in practice, and don't try any new lines that may suddenly appear to you.

Trailquest: Preparation is at least 50% of the skill of a trailquest event. Bring the right equipment and know how to use it properly – then all you have to do is pedal. Being capable of reading a map is a pretty basic requirement.

A-Z of biking terms

Aheadset
The trade name of a newer design of headset, which uses an unthreaded steerer tube. The stem clamps on externally (see expander wedge).

Allen key
Hexagonal drive bar, in various sizes, that fits into the head of an Allen bolt. Most bikes use Allen bolts.

Anodising
Treatment process that colours or hardens the surface of aluminum.

Bar ends
Bolt-on extensions to your handlebars, that give you extra, more powerful positions to climb or cruise with.

Bearings
The round balls that rotate on bearing surfaces inside your hubs and bottom brackets.

Bolt circle diameter (BCD)
The diameter of the circle drawn through the center of the chainring bolts. Important to know when ordering replacements.

Boss
A frame fitting that's welded directly to the frame tubes.

Bottom bracket
The bearing that the cranks spin on, held in the bottom bracket shell.

Brazing
A frame construction technique using brass to join tubes together.

Bunny hop
Lifting the bike clear of the ground by pulling up on the bars and pedals.

Butting
A metal component that has the wall thickness or section increased in a step is said to be butted.

Cadence
The rate (in revs/sec) that you pedal at.

Cantilevers
The brakes that are typically fitted to all mountain bikes. They run on pivots welded to the forks or rear stays.

Cartridge bearings
A sealed bearing unit that pops into a shell, containing the bearing surfaces, ball bearings, grease and dirt seals.

Chainstays
The frame tubes that run from the bottom bracket shell to the rear dropout.

Chainrings
The cogs (usually three) fitted to the chainset. They increase in size from the inner to the outer.

Chainset
The complete assembly of crank, chain rings and bottom bracket.

Chain suck
When the chain ring refuses to let go of the chain, the chain gets sucked between the chainset and chainstay, usually causing damage.

Chromoly
A high strength steel alloy used in bicycle frame construction.

Cleat
A hardened metal plate that clips into a clipless pedal's mechanism, locking the shoe to it.

Cogs
The cogs are at the rear of the bike and driven by the chain.

Crank
The metal arms that run from the pedal to the bottom bracket axle.

Crank extractor
Specialist tool for removing crank arms.

Damping
A speed sensitive system which uses oil to control the movement of a suspension system.

Derailleur
The mechanism that pushes the chain across the cogss or chainwheels, when a shift lever is moved.

Dish
The amount a wheel is offset on the hub. A rear wheel is dished to give room for the cogs.

Disk brake
A braking system that works on a disc mounted to the hub, rather than working on the rim.

Double butted
A tube that has greater wall thickness at both ends than in the middle section.

Down tube
The frame tube that runs from the bottom of the head tube to the the bottom bracket.

Dropout
The plate welded to the frame or forks, where the wheels locate into the frame.

Elastomers
Synthetic rubbers that have elastic properties. Used in suspension forks as a spring and damping medium.

Endo
A trick involving rocking your bike forwards on it's front wheel by locking the front wheel.

Expander wedge
Used to jam the traditional stem inside the steerer tube of the fork (see Aheadset).

Flange
The part of the hub the spokes thread through.

Forks
The part of the bike that holds the front wheel, and turns to allow steering.

Freewheel
Cunningly designed hub that lets the wheel go on turning when you stop pedalling.

Front derailleur
The gear mechanism that shifts the chain across the chainwheels.

Gear ratio
A method of determining the gearing of the bike, measured in effective wheel diameter.

Granny ring
The smallest chainring.

Gripshift
A type of gear changing system relying on twist-grip activation.

Groupset
The core of the bike's components. Gears, brakes, hubs, bearings, cranks, headset.

Handlebar
The part of the bike that your grips, shifters and levers mount to.

Head tube
The short tube that runs from the top of the forks to the bottom of the stem. Contains the headset.

Headset
The bearing in which the fork steerer tube rotates, contained in the headtube.

Hub
The unit that holds the bearings, and supports the spokes at the center of the wheel.

Hyperglide
Brand name of Shimano rear gear cogs which have profiled teeth and special shift ramps for easier shifting under load.

Indexing
Gears which click from position to position, making selecting the right one easy.

Jockey wheels
The two small wheels which guide the chain in the rear derailleur.

Knobblies
Aggressive tyres for true off road use.

Lacing
The process or type of spoking pattern used on wheels.

Lube
Anything from oil to heavy duty grease. Dry lubes evaporate leaving a dry film (usually based on teflon). Wet lubes remain wet to the touch and protect better in wet conditions. Dry lubes are good for dusty conditions because they don't pick up dirt.

Nipple
Small brass or alloy threaded adjuster that fixes the spokes to the rim.

Nylock
A nut with a nylon insert which the bolt thread cuts into, designed to stop the nut working loose.

Presta
The thin valve, used more commonly on racing bikes, and the choice for some offroad riders.

Quick Release (QR)
A mechanism that allows quick and easy tightening usually of the wheel hub/axle assembly and the seat post clamp.

Rapidfire
A type of shifter, made by Shimano, which operates with two levers, one moving the chain to a smaller cog, and the other moving it to a larger cog.

Rear derailleurs
The gear mechanism that moves the chain across the rear cogs.

Rim
The metal hoop of the wheel, and that the tyre runs on.

Schrader
A type of valve used on cars and some mountain bikes.

Seat stays
The frame tubes that run from where the seat post enters the frame to the rear dropouts.

Seat post
The tube that supports the saddle.

Seat tube
The tube that holds the seatpost and runs down to the bottom bracket.

Shifters
The levers on the handlebars to allow you to change gear.

Shimano
The Japanese component manufacturer which has almost total market dominance on production bikes. Makes good reliable equipment.

Slider
The moving part of a suspension fork leg.

Spokes
The thin metal cables that run from the hub to the rim.

Spoke key
Tool which turns spoke nipples and adjusts spoke tension. A wheel wrecker in the wrong hands.

Stanchion
The fixed part of a suspension fork leg.

Steerer tube
The tube that runs inside the head tube, locating the headset and supporting the front fork.

Stem
The welded tube assembly that connects the handlebar to the front fork.

Top tube
The horizontal frame tube that runs from the top of the head tube to the top of the seat tube.

Truing
The process of straightening a wheel by adjusting the tension of the spokes.

Wheelbase
The distance between the front and rear axles.

Index

ACKNOWLEDGEMENTS

The authors would like to thank **Trek Bicycle Corporation** for their support
during the production of this book.

Cooling Brown would also like to thank the following:

Nick Fish at Trek for his commitment to the project;

Jill Behr at Stockfile for all her useful advice;

Tim Marsh, **Gayle Lancaster** and **Dave Hemmings** for acting as models;

Apex Cyles (40 Clapham High Street, London SW4) &

Brixton Cycles (435 Coldharbour Lane, London SW9) for the loan of equipment;

Indexing Specialists for the index and **Dan Thisdell** for his editorial assistance.